T0121969

You Never

Know

A Memoir

PHILIP ZEID

BALBOA.
PRESS

A DIVISION OF HAY HOUSE

Balboa Press books may be ordered through booksellers or by contacting:

Balboa Press
A Division of Hay House
1663 Liberty Drive
Bloomington, IN 47403
www.balboapress.com.au
1 (877) 407-4847

Because of the dynamic nature of the Internet, any web addresses or links contained in this book may have changed since publication and may no longer be valid. The views expressed in this work are solely those of the author and do not necessarily reflect the views of the publisher, and the publisher hereby disclaims any responsibility for them.

The author of this book does not dispense medical advice or prescribe the use of any technique as a form of treatment for physical, emotional, or medical problems without the advice of a physician, either directly or indirectly. The intent of the author is only to offer information of a general nature to help you in your quest for emotional and spiritual well-being. In the event you use any of the information in this book for yourself, which is your constitutional right, the author and the publisher assume no responsibility for your actions.

Any people depicted in stock imagery provided by Thinkstock are models, and such images are being used for illustrative purposes only. Certain stock imagery © Thinkstock.

Print information available on the last page.

ISBN: 978-1-4525-3161-8 (sc)
ISBN: 978-1-4525-3162-5 (e)

Balboa Press rev. date: 11/07/2015

I dedicate this book to my dear wife, Nina who, during our married life, was my greatest friend and companion. Prior to our marriage she had never been out of New South Wales yet adapted so well to so many new, unfamiliar and dangerous situations and at the same time managed to bring up a wonderful family of five children.

CONTENTS

Introduction ix

Part 1 A Civilian Bachelor's Life 1
Part 2 Married Life... 53
Part 3 The War Period 111

INTRODUCTION

During our lives we do many things, in some cases apparently trivial, and make many choices completely unaware or oblivious of the profound effect they might have on our future. Likewise, many events take place in the world around us which at the time may seem unconnected to our future. These events may also be trivial or they may be world-shaking. How will such events affect our lives?

You never know.

I will begin my story from the time I was demobilised from the Royal Air Force and leave discussing my six years war service till last.

PART 1

A CIVILIAN BACHELOR'S LIFE

A short time after my demobilisation from the Royal Air Force my friend, who had been posted to Japan and had now also been demobilised, contacted me. An uncle of his had a 15 ton yacht, called Chinkara, lying in Bosham harbour on the south coast of England. It had been laid up during the war. The deck needed recalking, mast stepped and rigged and generally refitted. He asked me if I would be willing to help him get the yacht into shipshape condition and then go sailing in the English Channel with him, his uncle, his sister and her girlfriend. Who could refuse such an offer? In no time I arrived to stay with him in Bosham. We spent several days recalking the deck using oakum and tar. The mast was lying along the deck and had to be stepped. We approached one of the dockside crane operators and asked him, if we brought the boat along side, would he lift the mast into position. "Sure" he said. "Bring it along side any time I am here". We waited for a suitable tide. Then with the yacht in tow we rowed up to the crane, anchored the boat and had the mast lifted into position. Then we towed it back to its berth and attached new rigging. Our only failure was our inability to get the engine to work. Our main problem was lack of spare parts. Without an engine, our sailing skills would be taxed to the limit particularly when entering, berthing and leaving harbour. The two of us alone did all the work and were the crew during our forthcoming cruise in the English Channel.

Over the next few weeks my friend's sister, her girl friend and my friend's elderly uncle, all five of us, sailed to France, around the Channel Islands and the south coast of England. It was quite a feat as we did all this using only a hand held compass and a school atlas. We also, as mentioned earlier, did it without the use of the engine. Sailing in the English Channel was a most relaxing and exhilarating adventure. Two ports of call, which required great sailing skill to enter especially without an engine, were Yarmouth on the Isle of Wight and Cherbourg in France. The former had a narrow entrance through which could flow strong tides. When we arrived there we saw a power boat aground at the entrance. We entered the harbour, dropped our sails at the appropriate time and drifted slowly up to our berth.

Cherbourg has a long narrow entrance with high walls on each side and very little room to manoeuvre, especially a yacht under sail, yet we managed to enter, berth and depart safely. On one occasion, on a stormy night, when trying to enter Le Havre with sails reefed, in heavy seas and lashing rain and a strong headwind we tried for several hours to enter the Seine River but could make no headway. Eventual we realised we were not only fighting against the wind but also the flow of the river. We gave up and sailed into the darkness awaiting the storm to die down. If we had proper charts and tide tables we would have known how to avoid this problem. Crossing the triangle made by the French coast and the Cherbourg peninsula, our keel scraped the bottom. Later we noticed a slight leak but we were fortunate that there were no shallower areas in the vicinity. Again this shows the wisdom of having good charts.

My future career.

During the war, apart from operating in Burma, I had spent some time in North East India and Assam. During that time I had met several Tea Planters and ever since had been keen on taking up a career as a Tea Planter. At the end of the war I was entitled to be demobilised immediately in order to resume my studies at University. In view of my war time experiences I could not imagine returning to a life of study. So I refused this offer and remained in the Air Force until my demobilisation six months later. On demobilisation the Government offered Ex-Servicemen courses that would help them take up a suitable career or occupation in civilian life. With the idea of becoming a Tea Planter, I applied for a one year Diploma Course in Tropical Agriculture at the North of Scotland College of Agriculture attached to Aberdeen University.

Coinciding with the completion of the course, Partition Riots broke out in India so no Plantation jobs were available there.

A friend told me of an opening for a Rubber Planting job in Malaya, as it was then known. I applied for it and was asked to come for an immediate interview. The next day I travelled from Scotland down to London. I obviously made a good impression as I was accepted on the spot or perhaps they were short of applicants? - I was informed that my first tour of duty would be for five years during which time marriage was not allowed. Unbeknown to me accepting this job would prove to be one of the most fortunate decisions I could have made. Within a few days I was inoculated, vaccinated, packed and ready to fly to the far away Malay Peninsular. One small case contained my worldly possessions.

If it had not been for the partition riots in India, I would have become a Tea Planter in India and my life would have taken a different direction. Now I was to become a rubber planter in Malaya and a career in a country that I had never even thought of.

Amongst those I bade farewell before departing was my brother in-law, Sam, who was a doctor. On other occasions, when I had visited him at his surgery, there would be no more than half a dozen patients in his waiting room. The day I arrived the waiting room was full and there was a queue outside of at least twenty or thirty people also waiting to be seen. The receptionist knew who I was. When I told her my mission she let me in to say my farewells as soon as the patient being attended to had come out of the surgery. I asked Sam what was going on. He said it had been like this for the last few days, ever since the new free health scheme had started. My departure oversees coincided with the start of this scheme. As I knew I was going overseas I never joined. I thought to myself. How can free medical treatment and free medicine cause so much sickness?

Malaya.

I arrived in Malaya on 15th July 1948 and found that a State of Emergency had recently been declared because of an outbreak of terrorism carried out mainly by a few Chinese whose sympathies lay with the Chinese Communist Government. During the war a large number of Chinese had gone into the jungle to fight a guerrilla action against the occupying Japanese forces. Some were trained by British officers who had arrived in Malaya by submarine or air drops. Many of these Chinese guerrillas had taken part in the Victory Parades held to celebrate the end of the war. Some had handed in their weapons and returned to civilian life but others had stacked their weapons away for possible future use. Later these people returned to the jungle to try to oust the British and take over the running of the country. Fortunately there was no love lost between these Chinese Communist Terrorists and the local Malays, who overwhelmingly rejected them.

So after 6 years in the armed forces I was once more living in dangerous conditions. The Emergency, as it was known, continued for the next 10 years. It officially ended in 1958 one year after Malaya was granted independence from Britain. During the whole of that time I was accompanied by two armed Malay bodyguards, travelled in armoured cars and for self-protection was provided with a Reising sub-machine gun and .45 pistol.

My Job.

Apart from learning the job of being a planter it was necessary to learn to speak Malay and compulsory to learn Tamil as over 95% of the work force spoke only that language. There was a written and oral Tamil language test to be taken at the end of our first tour. If we did not pass this test we were not invited back for a subsequent tour of duty.

Our Company was the only American Company having rubber estates in Malaya. It owned six rubber Estates. The three largest were located in the northern State of Kedah, another was located in the State of Selangor and two in the State of Johor, one being in central Johor and the other in south Johor. It also operated a large plantation in Indonesia in North Sumatra, known by its initials, HAPM. The rubber estates covered a very large area of the Malay Peninsula. They varied in size from a few thousand acres up to over 10,000 acres or more. There was a small area set aside for the head office and housing for the manager and office staff. If the estate was large enough there would be a bungalow for an assistant or more. Near the head office of most Estates there would be shops selling basic necessities. On each division, which might be between 1000 and 1500 acres in size, there would be a bungalow for use by the assistant in charge of the division. There would also be housing for the workers, sometimes a small school, a dispensary, a crèche where children of workers were cared for while their mothers were at work. However the bulk of the area was planted with rubber. There would be a few small villages dotted here and there with estates occupying the intervening areas. Consequently the nearest neighbour might be as much as 5 miles away.

On arrival in Penang I stayed one night at the E & O hotel and on the next day I was posted to Dublin Estate in Kedah, an estate of about 10,000 acres. Without any previous experience or training, I was put in charge of Division four. The day I arrived at the office there was quite a commotion. The cause was a rabid dog which was foaming at the mouth, yelping hysterically - if dogs can be hysterical? and threatening the bystanders who were running around trying to keep away from this dangerous animal. It was quickly shot. Everyone was considerably relieved especially as no one had been bitten. It can be quite a shock when suddenly a normally behaved dog suddenly changes its self into a demon. It speaks well for the authorities that within two years of my arrival rabies had been eradicated from the whole country. A licencing system for all dogs was introduced. A small fee was charged for the dog to be licensed. Then the licensed dog was inoculated against rabies and tagged. Dog owners were given one year in which to licence their dogs and have them immunised after which time all unlicenced dogs would be shot. The license tags were quite large and visible. Throughout the country dog shooters were engaged. When the time to license dogs had expired, it was their duty to round up all unlicensed stray dogs and shoot them. For some time afterwards you would occasionally hear yelping of dogs followed by gunshots then silence. This operation lasted just over a year. The result was that within this time the country became free of rabies. I never saw another rabid dog again.

For security reasons, the Assistant bungalows on each Division were not used. During the Emergency, we were all located in the safest areas on the estate, which was usually the area around head office. This required us to share bungalows. On Dublin Estate I was sharing a bungalow with a pre war planter. He provided me with transport to and from my Division. I was told that in due course I would get a company car.

My first word in Tamil.

It was my second day on the Division. A dispute had arisen between two rubber tappers. The rubber tapper is the person who harvests the rubber from the rubber tree by making a sloping incision into the bark, but not so deep as to wound the cambium. The cambium is the growing area that lies between the wood and bark of the tree. The latex then flows down this cut and into a cup, placed below a spout, where it is collected.

Latex harvested from rubber tree.

Toddy is made from fermented Palm juice. The Toddy tapper, as he is called, would climb the palm in the morning and shave off a thin slice from the growing shoot. Palm syrup would flow from the cut and be collected in an earthenware pot placed below the cut. It would be collected before midday and poured into vats. Fermentation would rapidly occur and by late afternoon it was a potent alcoholic drink. This was the local "beer". It was quite cheap and was consumed in the estate "Toddy Shop" in the late afternoon or early evening. Each day an Assistant would be assigned the job of ensuring that the remaining toddy was thrown out at day's end, as if left, it would become very potent and, later, dangerous to drink,

Back to my story. There were two Rubber Tappers who were the best of friends and spent most afternoons and evenings in the "Toddy" shop drinking together. One of them had a daughter and the other a son. The two had eloped which in itself at the time was more than outrageous. The families were Hindu and normally would be considered to be of the same caste. However, when their children ran off together the small caste difference between them, which previously had been of no consequence, reared its ugly head. They were now no longer friends and had both come to me for judgment and a ruling on their dispute. As the Assistant it was my duty to hear the evidence and then, as both judge and jury, pronounce judgment. I was called upon to resolve the situation. At that time I spoke no Tamil and had only been in my present position of authority for two days. I had no idea of the procedure to follow and I had to have an interpreter. The Supervisor, locally known as a Conductor, whose name was Pillai, served as my Interpreter. I learned later that what usually happened was

9

that each litigant would be required to briefly state his case after which the Assistant would make an instant decision. The whole affair would be over in quick time. I did not know this and proceeded to hear each person's side of the story in great detail – nodding wisely as they spoke as if I understood all they were saying before it was interpreted to me. I even went so far, through my interpreter, as to interrogate them on certain points. Something I later learned was unheard of. When everything they had to say had been said, I was faced with the predicament of not knowing how to resolve such a difficult case. After hearing all the evidence they stood silently before me expecting an immediate decision. In my mind's eye I envisioned them as eager supplicants standing before me, their judge, head bowed cap-in-hand waiting for a momentous decision. Of course there was no cap-in-hand they both wore rather old cloths wound around their heads. What decision was there to make? My mind was a blank and I was in a state of confusion. So I decided to play for time. I told them, through my interpreter, that in view of the complexity of the case I would have to take the matter under consideration and deliver my verdict the next day. In order to provide the greatest effect I thought I should say something in Tamil. I asked the Conductor what tomorrow was in Tamil and was told it was "Narlikki". So with great gravity I spoke the first word I was to learn in Tamil - "Narlikki". I then rose from my seat, indicating that the case was postponed till the following day.

I spent a worrisome night wondering what possible solution there could be to such a problem. The next day I arrived at the office at the usual time of 3.00 pm, after the day's work had been completed, still with no solution in mind.

The two parties were brought in. Before I had time to say a word they both broke out speaking in rapid Tamil. At last they calmed down and I was able to ask the Conductor what all this was about. Imagine my amazement to learn that they were praising my judgment. They considered me to be a wise councillor and thanked me for my infinite patience and wisdom in resolving, in such a magnificent manner, what must have been one of the Division's most important and difficult cases ever. Once more they were the best of friends. I am not sure which was the most dominant of my emotions, amazement, or relief, that the case was closed without requiring my intervention.

I found out later what had happened. They left the office thrilled and proud that they had had such a long hearing and that their case was so important that judgment could not, as usual, be made on the spur of the moment. The facts as presented by them were being carefully considered by the *sinna Dore* (the junior Assistant) and a decision was to be made the following day. This information quickly spread throughout the workforce, who were equally proud to be part of this great happening. The two went off to the *Toddy* shop to celebrate their new found importance among their friends. The drinking re-bonded their friendship and this must have mellowed them to the point where they were pleased to accept their children as respectively daughter and son in law. Whilst in their cups they no doubt must have arrived at the conclusion that I, their wise new Assistant, was responsible for all this happening. From that day my reputation as a wise and fair task master was indelibly written in their minds and that of the whole division.

Linden Estate.

After only 2 weeks on Dublin Estate, our most northern estate, I was transferred to Linden Estate our most southern Estate. Our company had engaged, an American Security Officer who was also an Arms expert. The company had, on his recommendation and for our protection, purchased "White" armoured cars and weapons from America. The weapons were Riesing sub-machine-guns, .45 calbre pistols and Johnson rifles. The rifle was unique in that they had a round-shaped fixed irremovable magazine into which you could insert the familiar .303 bullet at any time. I had never come across this very useful and unique "top-up" system before. The rifles however were very heavy and not really suited for use by the smaller framed local Malays.

As terrorism spread throughout the country and became a more serious threat, the Malayan Government created an Auxiliary Police Force manned by Malays. The recruits were known as Special Constables. They had their own distinctive uniforms and were commonly referred to as SCs. Their duty was primarily to protect planters, miners and their families. They became personal bodyguards, and friends, two per assistant, and also were used to man, 24 hours a day, the pill boxes that were built around each bungalow. They needed training. So two weeks after my arrival on Dublin Estate I, with my previous wartime experience, was posted to Linden Estate, in South Johor, to train the special constables there in the use of weapons and at the same time learn how to become a planter. Later many ex-Palestine police were recruited to command the Special Constable units. Due to changes in the political situation in Palestine these men were no longer required there. It was fortunate that they were available to provide their expertise in taking over the command of the SC Units.

On Linden Estate I was to share the bungalow with the manager and his wife. There was an assistant's bungalow on the estate but it was some way off. As mentioned earlier it was too dangerous for individuals to occupy their own bungalow unless it was close by in the same compound. I still had no transport so the only way I could reach the more remote parts of the estate was to travel in the same truck that transported the Tamil workers. The rubber tappers made their own way to their allotted plot. So most times I travelled with the weeding gang who were usually women. The rear of the truck was full of women dressed in a variety of colourful working saris and all jabbering away in a language that I was expected to become fluent in. I could not return for morning refreshment so I took some sandwiches and a couple of bottles of beer with me each morning. I used to put the beer in a stream, which kept it beautifully cool. When the morning break was due I would sit down and enjoy my beer and sandwiches together with the workers. We had to pass a Tamil language exam at the end of our first tour of duty. If we did not pass this language test we would not be invited back for a second tour. This period therefore provided me with a wonderful opportunity to quickly improve my language skills and at the same time become well known to the ordinary workers

My Malay was very basic at that time, as we had to concentrate on learning Tamil. None of the Special Constables spoke any English. I was always interested in learning languages and spoke reasonable French, passable German and also a smattering of Hindustani, the latter which I learnt during the war while serving in the Far East. I soon learnt the limited vocabulary needed to carry out my role training the Malays Special Constables. One night, after several weeks into training, terrorists shot at our bungalow. The special constables responded in a very well organized fashion, firing back in a very disciplined manner. It was their first encounter and I was very pleased with how they responded to the night attack. I was very proud of them and wanted to tell them so. I looked up the word "proud" in the dictionary and there it was "*sombong*". In my best Malay I told them I was very proud of them - using the word "*sombong*". I continued to use this word, in that context, for some time to come. A little later I learned the Malay (slang) word for "express train". The locals called it "*Kereta Api Sombong*". Literally translated (carriage fire proud) "Proud Fire Carriage". The explanation was that the express train was too proud, haughty or conceited to stop at the smaller stations. It was then I realized the ambiguity of the word "proud". I was embarrassed to think of the occasions on which I used this word. I recalled how I had used it when I had praised my special constables some months earlier. I had, inadvertently, told them I was conceited. The Malays are a very polite people and would consider it the height of rudeness to correct any such error. They had not even indicated by gesture or looks that what I had said must have sounded very strange and amusing to them. So I added a new word to my vocabulary "*bangga*" which would have conveyed, in the correct manner, the feeling of pride I had for them at that time,

My Birth Mark.

Whilst on Linden Estate I became seriously ill. I contracted a high fever and at times was delirious. I recall lying on a bed, wet with perspiration and occasionally seeing faces peering down at me. They were probably the manager, the manager's wife and the Indian "Dresser" or all three. Nowadays we would call the "Dresser" a paramedic. He, between the visiting European doctor's weekly calls, took care of the minor medical needs of the workforce. My illness turned out to be dengue fever. I believe it is also called bone wrack fever. From its name you can guess it is very painful. I recall complaining to the Dresser of one particular painful spot on my back. He said he had the solution. He would "cup" it and draw out the pain. He took a glass and a strip of paper. He lit the paper, put the flame in the glass, to burn up the oxygen and expand the air and then placed the glass on my bare flesh over the agonising spot. What happens when the air in the glass contracts is that it sucks the flesh into the glass. I believe this is ideal for use on boils as it extracts the puss. But it did absolutely nothing to ease the excruciating pain I was experiencing.

As seemed customary in those days, hospital was only considered when all else had failed. The patient was by then probably on the road to recovery – or something worse. This is why, for some time to come Hospitals had such a bad reputation among the locals. Only the dead and dying were brought there. In my case "All Else" had failed. So in a weak and exhausted condition I was bundled off to the Johor General Hospital only 25 miles away in Johor Bahru. However, I was already on the road to recovery so I was not there very long. Prior to my discharge one of the nurses told me that I had the most remarkable and perfect birthmark on my back that she had ever seen. I told her I had no such birthmark or I would have known. She insisted I had. She produced a mirror and showed me. There, on my back, plain for all to see was a perfectly rounded red birthmark. For a moment I was stunned. To have such a mark there all my life and not know! How was this possible? Then I recalled the "cupping" I explained it to the nurse and we both had a good chuckle. The blood vessels, damaged by the cupping, later healed and my "birthmark" disappeared.

About two months after this "cupping" incident the "Dresser" came to a sad end. The bungalows provided were raised off the ground and had a verandah around them. The Dresser's favourite evening pastime was to sit on the verandah and consume vast quantities of toddy. One evening in a drunken stupor he must have leant on the railings around the verandah which gave way. He fell some distance to the ground and was killed.

Scarboro Estate.

Mechanical Replanting.

I had completed training the SCs (Special Constables) on Linden Estate and was settling into the routine of being a planter when I was transferred back to Kedah. Around that time the company decided to embark on a replanting program of our oldest rubber trees which were located on Scarboro Estate, Kedah. The idea was to carry out Mechanical Replanting using tractors. I was selected to be the assistant-in-charge of the Replanting Unit under the supervision of a senior man located in our head office on Penang Island. As an added bonus I received the use of a car, two months earlier than normal; more about the car and my driving skills later.

The standard method of felling old rubber trees was by use of a Trewella winch. This was a slow and laborious method. The winch was attached to the base of a standing tree and heavy cables attached high up on the tree to be felled. A lever and ratchet system was operated by a worker and gradually the tree to be felled would be pulled out of the vertical until it fell to the ground. Then, followed the job of cutting it up and burning it. The company decided to do away with this manual device and replace it with tractors. They purchased three Allis Chalmers 20 ton tractors and two smaller D8 Caterpillars. We engaged a very competent Indian mechanic from whom I learned a lot. With the use of a special attachment, fitted to the front of the tractor, we were able to fell trees at a very high rate and also to stack them into windrows for later burning. We found out very quickly that we could not use them in very wet weather. They easily got bogged and in such conditions also ruined the texture of the soil. Other than that they were ideal for the purpose in hand. So we only used them in suitable weather conditions. I learned to carry out all repairs, drive them, fell trees, to weld and spray paint. Most important was that I kept detailed records of all repairs and maintenance. This was to prove invaluable later and probably was partly responsible for my promotion within the company at a faster rate than expected.

My First Car.

Having been provided with a car presented me with a problem. The problem was that I had never driven a car before. However, I did have a driving licence. How I came by this is interesting. During the war we were allowed to apply for a driving licence without having to pass a driving test. I am not sure if this only applied to service personnel. I had never driven a car; nevertheless I applied for a driving licence which was immediately granted. If I recall correctly it cost me five shillings. At the end of the war there were an excessive number of drivers, like myself, who needed to be tested. Consequently the Government gave all holders of such licences one year's grace in which to apply for a proper licence without having to pass a driving test. I applied and that is how I got my driving licence.

When I arrived in Malaya I applied for a Malayan driving license and produced my UK license as proof of my ability to drive a vehicle. On the application form I put in" ALL" and lo and behold, I was granted a license permitting me to drive every vehicle available. I held such a license all the time I was in Malaya. When I used it to obtain a license in Australia I only got permission to drive a car.

So how did I manage to drive my first car in Malaya? On Scarboro Estate, where I was posted, there was an air strip which had been put in by the Japanese during the war. My friend, Alan, the other assistant on Scarboro, with whom I shared a bungalow, took me to the airstrip in his car and showed me how to start, stop, change gears and drive up and down the air strip. The airstrip was wide, long and flat, ideally suited for a beginner. Along the side of the airstrip were bunkers constructed from laterite where the Japanese Aircraft could be safely kept when not in use to protect them from being damaged in the event of a bombing attack. For a few days I periodically drove up and down the airstrip, changing gears, driving at various speeds, doing turns and becoming familiar with the vehicle. No automatics in those days.

When it was considered that I was a proficient enough driver we arranged that I pick up my car from Penang. Alan drove me to Penang where I took delivery of my car. Fortunately in those days there was hardly any traffic on the roads. In fact I believe the total number of registered vehicles on the mainland was less than 1000. So it was fairly easy and safe for me to drive from Penang to our estate bungalow. The main obstacle was the ferry which took us from the mainland to the island and back. In those early days the ferry was a modified tank landing craft. We drove to the Butterworth ferry terminal, on the mainland, and waited for the ferry to arrive to take us to Penang Island. The ferry arrived, slowed down, approached the wharf, docked and then let its wide front grey boarding ramp down allowing us to embark. Alan drove onto the ferry. We disembarked on the Penang side then proceeded to pick up my car. When we arrived back at the Penang terminal, Alan drove his car on to the ferry then came back and drove my car on. When we disembarked on the mainland we repeated the process. Then Alan proceeded at a reasonable pace all the way back to the estate with me following closely behind. I thought it would not take me long to become a proficient driver.

For two weeks I had been the proud owner of a new car but had not had the opportunity to drive it anywhere except on the gravel roads on the rubber estate. I was very disappointed that so far I had no opportunity to test my newly acquired driving skills on the government roads used by other drivers. Then one morning we received an invitation to a party to be held on our neighbouring Estate, Harvard, about 30 miles away. At last the opportunity to test my driving skills had arrived. That afternoon we left our bungalow, I driving my car and Alan following behind in his, to make sure all went well. On reaching the office it suddenly dawned on me that we would be driving back in the dark, something I had never done before. From past experience I knew the party would be a wild one and none of us would remain sober. My better judgment told me that even driving back in the dark sober would be a challenge let alone driving back in an inebriated state, which could be suicidal. Being the sensible person I am, I stopped at the office, Alan following suit. I told him of my concern. He agreed that, indeed, it would be wise that we should go in his car with him driving and that I should leave my car at the Estate office and pick it up on the way back. I closed all the windows of my car, locked the door climbed into Alan's car and off we drove to the party.

The party was a great success. All parties we attended were a great success, probably because of the vast amount of alcohol consumed. Having thoroughly enjoyed ourselves we left at about 1.30 a.m. for home. Arriving at the office we stopped so that I could pick up my car. I was full of confidence as well as drink. I got into the car, switched on the engine and headlights, and without even bothering to open the windows drove off like a bat out of hell, leaving Alan to follow. I remember my headlights lighting up the rubber trees on either side of the gravel road, rows and rows of tall silent sentinels waiting patiently for the dawn. Racing down the slope towards a bridge I confidently turned the steering wheel to guide my speeding chariot over the bridge. Imagine my amazement when the car did no such thing but continued in its original direction, skidding over the gravel road, missing a few rubber trees and flying gracefully into the air to land bonnet first into the water of the murky river that flowed under the bridge. An amazing thing happened. It was like being in a dream in wonderland. All the controls on the dashboard of my car, a Vauxhall Velox, operated by being pulled out towards the driver. The force of the impact on the front of the car pushed the dashboard back and switched everything on. I had interior lighting, radio and full beam headlights. The front of the car went down rapidly, but the rear of the car was lifted upwards mainly because of the air in the boot. The air in the passenger compartment could only leak out slowly because all the windows were shut. In my beautifully lit "cockpit" I noticed the water coming up through the clutch and accelerator pedals. I remember thinking it was time to get out of here. Then, sitting in my brand new vehicle below the surface of the river, I heard a small voice calling my name. "Phil, Phil", it cried. No time to wonder what that was all about. In my beautifully lit vehicle I saw the gleam of the right door handle. I grabbed it and tried to open the driver's door but it was stuck. I moved over to open the front passenger door it was also stuck. By that time I noticed the shining, slowly rising, horizontal lake of water had risen up to my waist. I remember quite distinctly thinking that if my life ended here I couldn't complain as I had had not only a fortunate life but an extremely interesting and lucky one. So I hopped over the back seat and tried to open the back door. I think enough water had got into the car, under pressure, to help the door open. I grabbed the car, and managed get onto the roof and stood there almost knee-deep as the murky muddy water flowed past. Who should be on the bridge but Alan, leaning on the rails, clearly silhouetted by the lights from his still running car parked behind him. It was Alan who had been calling out my name.

As he approached the bridge he saw brilliant lights under the murky water and stopped to investigate. When he realised it was my car, he had called out to me. When I emerged from the car and was standing on the car roof he asked me if I was all right. I shouted at him asking why the hell he had not jumped in to try and rescue me. His reply (and this is the unexaggerated truth) was "I had my new trousers on". Sopping wet, I got into his car and we drove home to get a good nights sleep.

Next day I realised how lucky I had been. The river I had gone into was about 10 feet deep and was usually almost dry. The night before we had a flash flood and the river was full. If it had been in its usual state I might not have survived or at the best been severely injured. The river was wide enough so that at the high speed I was travelling I still could not reach the opposite bank. The cushioning effect of the water reduced the effect of the impact. I got away with nothing more than bruised knees. When I had first got into the car I had not opened the windows. This had prevented the water rushing into the car and this had given me quite a bit of extra time to get out before the interior of the car became flooded.. The front doors did not open because the metal on either side of the engine bonnet had been pushed back by the impact and prevented them opening.

Later the next day when we went to see how we could retrieve the car. The river level had dropped considerably and there it was partially under water with all the lights still on and with a crowed of curious local onlookers. We got the car out by bulldozing a slope in the river bank with a tractor, diving in and tying a rope around the rear axle and pulling the car out.

Partly recovered car.

I had of course to report the loss of the car to the General Manager who called me in to his office in Penang and asked me to explain how, after only two weeks, I had wrecked the car. He was not amused at my half hearted explanation. He said he would think about providing me with a second car but it would not be for at least six months. I soon was able to save enough money, out of my meager wages, to buy an ex army BSA 250cc motor cycle. I used this till I was granted a new car. I recall that the motor cycle cost me the magnificent sum of M$75 Malayan dollars. The exchange rate at that time was about $8.40 to the pound Sterling. I had two dogs Sandy and McDuff. I taught them to accompany me on my motor bike. Sandy would sit on the petrol tank in front of me and McDuff sat on the pillion seat behind. I took them wherever I went on the Estate.

Buyer Beware.

There is a sequel to this story involving my car, which I had sunk in the river. The car had been pronounced a complete write-off. It was taken away and I never thought I would see it again. However a few months later when Maurice, my neighbour, and I were visiting Penang we noticed my car in the display window of one of the reputable car dealers. I knew it was mine by its number plate. We went in to make inquiries about it as it was up for sale as a secondhand car. The salesman came over and we made an inspection of the car. When I had it, its colour was green. It had been repainted. Now it was black. It had new upholstery. The mileage on the clock was just over 250 miles. This, as far as I could recall, was about right. We asked the salesman who the previous owner had been and why it was being sold with such a low mileage. We were told it had been owned by a wealthy elderly woman who was a very careful driver. On purchasing the car she found it too small for her needs and wished to exchange it for a larger one. We said the car looked as though it had been in an accident and been repainted. He denied this possibility. In those days the registration license on the front of the car included its colour and, there plain for all to see, was written the colour "green". He had no explanation for that so we left him to stew in his own embarrassment. The moral? Buyer beware!

My magnificent salary.

When I took up employment as a rubber planter the salary offered was thirty pounds a month. At the time I applied for the job in UK it seemed to be a very reasonable sum since accommodation was included. When I arrived in Malaya I found it was equivalent to about 250 Malay dollars a month. This turned out to be very difficult to live on. I discovered that this was a pre-war salary which did not match post-war costs. I was further financially embarrassed because it was essential to employ an Amah to do the cooking, laundry, and general cleaning of the bungalow. On top of this, 10% of our salary was deducted and placed in a Provident Fund against retirement. The least we could pay our employee was $60.00.a month. So out of my measly salary of $250.00 came $85.00 leaving $165.00 per month to cover food and all other expenses.

The Amah

The Amahs were Chinese females and a sect of their own. The ones we had were usually middle aged and dressed in a distinctive uniform. This consisted of a stiff white cotton top done up at the neck and wide black trousers made with some shiny material. They belonged to a Kongsi House or Clan House where they could reside and be looked after when unemployed or sick. None seemed to have husbands though some mentioned their children. They must have been left over from pre-war because as time went by they eventually disappeared from the scene. Their name was always preceded by an "Ah" which may have been the equivalent of our "Ms".

My Amah's name was Ah Kim. She looked after me as if I were her son. She was very bossy. She did all my shopping. She told me that if I did it I would be cheated but not her as she knew how much everything cost. She was absolutely right. When my shorts were getting worn and frayed she told me to get some new ones as she was losing face. When I told her I could not afford new ones she went out and bought some cloth and made them for me on her sewing machine. She only charged me for the cost of the material.

My Dogs.

Ah Kim must have been one of the most tolerant Amahs one could wish for. I had accumulated five dogs all of them mongrels. However, one of them was larger than the others and looked very much like an Alsatian. They usually slept on my bed. At night, at the least noise outside, they would all, in unison, run outside, yelping, to see what was going on. Having satisfied their curiosity they would return to my bed and carry on sleeping. The soil around the bungalow was laterite, a reddish coloured earth, and if the soil was wet or if it was raining, the dogs would return to my bed wet and covered in laterite. Ah Kim only mildly complained but willingly continued to do the extra laundry caused by my dogs' outrageous behaviour.

The bungalow I lived in was built pre-war and was made of wood. It had a raised floor which was on stilts. This helped to keep the building very cool. However, because the bungalows had been neglected during the war, they were in a very dilapidated condition. This was well illustrated by the fact that later, when another Planter was sharing a meal with me, the floor under his chair gave way and he nearly disappeared through the hole

In spite of Ah Kim's efforts it was very difficult to make ends meet. I frequently went hunting wild pig, sometimes with the Tamil tappers who used dogs and spears. Because of the emergency I was a fully armed and so my Tamil tappers were always assured of a sufficient supply of wild pig if I accompanied them. The wild pig was a vicious brute, extremely strong and dangerous. Its meat had very little fat and had a very strong flavour. It was however, excellent in a curry. Also, to supplement my food supply, I started raising chickens for meat and eggs. My house became full of breeding boxes as I took every opportunity to increase my flock. It was not long before I had dozens of chickens all over the place. During the day they would go foraging in the rubber Plantation. When I got back from early morning work I would give them a feed of *Padi,* (the Malay name for rice with the husk still on). With cries of" CHOOK chook chook chook" they would come rushing from all directions, out of the rubber, to be fed with the rice I threw to them. At night they would return to their roosts in or near the bungalow. They provided me with eggs and more often than not Chicken was on the menu.

We did not move around too much at night because of the existing emergency even though we were at all times fully armed and carried our weapons wherever we went. This included times we visited shops, restaurants, the bank and all other such places. Therefore shared meals and entertainment mostly occurred during the day. However, sometimes close neighbours would brave an early evening meal. Maurice, my closest neighbour was a frequent visitor as I was to him.

I recall one evening when we had finished our meal and consumed our fair share of drink that a rat appeared. This in itself was not unusual. However, on this occasion it scurried along the skirting board and then had the cheek to stop and look at us. "Let's get it" I whispered. In unison we pulled out our guns and shot it dead. A few more holes in a dilapidated bungalow would not be noticed.

The Tottie (pronounced Toh tee).

I recalled that when we were in our late teens and still at school, my brother and I attempted to make some orange wine. With this past experience in mind I now decided that I would make some potato wine. If successful I intended to distil it to turn it into Pocheen or a type of Vodka. I obtained two large glass demijohns in which to make the brew. These jars were used to store formic acid which was used to coagulate latex to make rubber sheets. I purchased the required amount of sugar and potatoes. The sliced potatoes were placed in the jars together with the sugar. The jars were then filled with water and covered with clean cloth to prevent contamination. I could not obtain yeast but hoped that fermentation would start spontaneously. I waited several days inspecting the bottles several times a day looking for the tell tale bubbles that come when fermentation starts. Nothing happened. I was considering throwing the batch away and starting all over again when a brilliant idea struck me. The palm juice, from which Toddy was made, commenced fermenting immediately and vigourously as soon as it was harvested. It was like nothing I had ever seen before. What if I put a small amount of Toddy in each jar? Would it start the fermentation process? It certainly did. The next day my two jars were bubbling away like mad. This I thought was a tribute to lateral thinking. In a few days the fermentation process slowed down and finally I was able to bottle the brew. I placed my valuable treasure of bottled potential potato wine in a cool place with wet sacking placed over the bottles in case any blew up. I then waited patiently for about 3 weeks before sampling the wine.

At long last the day for sampling my precious brew arrived. I opened the first bottle and was pleased to hear the sound associated with released gas under pressure. I poured this sparkling brew into a glass and sampled it. It tasted exactly like Toddy, but first class Toddy. I had previously tasted Toddy to see if I would like it. I found I could not stomach the stuff and thoroughly disliked it. So here was I with gallons of first rate Toddy, which I could not drink. My plan to make Pocheen had failed. What to do?

It was about 9.30 in the morning just after I had returned home after completing my morning duties and had just finished my breakfast. It happened that this was the time and day that the Tottie did his rounds which included my bungalow. In the Indian caste system the Tottie is allotted, by his Maker, the role of cleaning toilets, septic tanks, and all other menial cleaning jobs shunned by his fellow men. He was born into the system as a Tottie as were all other classes of workers born into theirs. However, in the more enlightened social society in Malaya, away from the strong cultural influences surrounding them in India, the younger generation were throwing off some of these restrictive customs of their Hindu religion. Sons of Totties were not prepared to follow in their father's footsteps. Therefore the few Totties remaining were very old. Mine was no exception. He was old, frail, thin boned, stooped and with wrinkle brown skin. He wore only a loin cloth and the customary turban made of an old piece of cloth which was wound around his skinny almost bald head. I knew he would be a toddy drinker. So I filled a beer glass of my brew which I offered to him. He was very reluctant to try it. Eventually I managed to convince him to try it. He took the glass; he hesitated; he eyed me suspiciously. Then, after a long pause, reluctantly took a small sip. There was another pause then with a *"rumba nallathe Dore"* (Its very good Sir) he sunk the lot. I asked him if he would like some more and he eagerly said yes - a very big change from his earlier suspicious attitude. So I told him I would leave several bottles for him to take home when he finished his work.

Early next morning the Divisional Conductor (Supervisor) came to my house asking to see me. He wanted to know if the Tottie had been here yesterday as he had not returned home last night. I told him yes he had been here. So the conductor left to seek out the Tottie elsewhere.

There had been and always were cases being reported of paralysis, blindness and even deaths caused by locals making and consuming or selling illegally brewed alcoholic drinks, locally known as *samsu*. I suddenly recalled this and started to imagine the poor old Tottie lying not just dead drunk but truly dead, somewhere in the rubber. The thought would not go away. I did not know what to do. I knew it would not be long before someone found him while tapping the rubber trees. Perhaps everything would be alright; perhaps not!

I knew however that I would have to get rid of my poisonous brew before any more damage could be done. I went off on my usual rounds wondering when the Tottie's fate would be known. If, by afternoon, no news was forthcoming I would have to report the incident and a search party would be organized to find him. At lunch time when work was finished I returned to my bungalow and poured the contents of all my bottles into the drain. Nothing was left. No one else would be poisoned. About half an hour later, just before I was ready to take the usual afternoon siesta I heard, in the distance, the sound of voices. I went out to investigate and there coming up the hill, from the "lines" (the divisional housing units) was a large group of workers. "Good God I thought." They have found the Tottie. He is dead and they are coming to lynch me. For the sake of my position I was duty bound to face them. They arrived, stopped, and their spokesman stepped forward. What was the news he was he bringing? What was going to happen now? Then he began to speak. This morning when we got back from work we found the Tottie had returned. He told us that you were giving away bottles of excellent Toddy. It was so potent that he had unwittingly over imbibed and fallen asleep drunk in the rubber. He only woke up in the morning. Your honour, if you are still giving away such a wonderful brew may we respectfully request you provide us with some. My relief new no bounds. Then I had to tell them that unfortunately I had no more. I had given the last bottles to the Tottie. I omitted of course telling them that I had thrown gallons of this wonderful brew away. What a great great pity. I would have gained enormous respect if I had kept my hoard and now distributed it to my faithful workers. Such is life.

My First Local Leave.

My nearest neighbour, when I arrived on Scarboro Estate, was Maurice, who I have mentioned before. He worked for another company and lived in a bungalow about five miles away. We had shared many experiences together and we were constant visitors to each others bungalows. We shared many a meal together. Maurice and I were to become the closest of and lifelong friends. Our wives, when we married and later our children, shared the same special close lifelong relationship. We would spend most of our holidays visiting one another. We were like family.

At the end of my first year of service (July 1949) I was due two weeks leave and so was Maurice. So Maurice and I decided to take this leave together and travel to Bangkok. We chose to go by rail for two reasons. One, we could only afford to go by train. Two, Maurice had been a prisoner of war (POW) at Kanchan Burri. The train passed through this village on its way to Bangkok. A Thai family had been very good to him when he was a POW and he wanted to take the opportunity to visit them. So we took Malayan Railways to Padang Besar in Perlis which is located on the Malaya/Siam (now Thailand) border. There we changed trains to travel the rest of the journey on the Thai railway. The first thing that drew our attention was the dilapidated conditions of the coaches. The wood could have done with a coat of vanish or paint and there were remnants of ash and soot everywhere. As soon as we started on our long journey we became aware of large quantities of soot and ash entering our compartment. The steam train was belching out prodigious amounts of soot and ash. We had the choice of closing all the windows and sweltering in the heat or leaving them open and putting up with the soot and ash. With the agreement of the other two occupants of the carriage we decided to leave the window slightly open.

We soon discovered the reason for this unusual situation. A short distance down the track we stopped. There was no station only jungle on either side. Looking out of the window we noted the firemen loading wood from a large neat pile stacked at the side of the jungle through which the train was travelling. Coal, at that time, was not available. The engine was burning wood. This produced the large quantities of smoke, soot and ash that we had to put up with. The wood burned quite quickly and we were constantly stopping to replenish fuel from more stocks of wood piled up along the side of the rail track by contractors employed by the railway.

Each meal during the journey consisted of bread, eggs and Asahi (Japanese) beer. The menu never changed. We had never heard of or tasted Asahi beer before but found it a very good beer. We drank it with pleasure knowing that it was much safer than risking drinking water from some unknown and probably contaminated source; a marvelous excuse for anyone traveling in the tropics

When we reached the first of the many rivers we were to cross we were in for another surprise. During the war all the major bridges between Padang Besar, the Malayan town at the Thai border, and Bangkok had been destroyed. We were forced to disembark and, with our meagre amount of luggage, take a *sampan* (local small open boat) across the river to another train waiting patiently for us on the other side. This process was repeated at every river crossing during our journey.

Blown-up Bridges in Thailand (Then Siam)

We finally arrived and disembarked at Kanchan Burri. Maurice obviously knew where to go in this small town and we soon arrived, unexpectedly and unannounced at the house of his wartime Thai friends. After getting over the initial shock of seeing such an unexpected visitor and his friend, we were greeted in the warmest fashion with hugs and lots of "Ahs" Then we squatted down to a meal and exchange of greetings mainly in sign language as I spoke not a word of Thai and Maurice was not very fluent. The family had several children. The youngest, at the time Maurice left the POW (Prisoner of War) Camp, must have been about 10 years old. She had grown quite a bit since then. They had called her Lik Lik which I believe, in Thai, means little one. She was still called by that name and that is the only Thai word I know.

The time arrived for us to leave our Thai friends and continue our rail journey to Bangkok. On arrival we found a suitable hotel. Bangkok, with its beautiful temples and distinctive architecture was a most interesting place and we enjoyed ourselves thoroughly. I had travelled extensively in Asia and had always found someone who understood and spoke English. Thailand, at the time of our visit, was an exception. The reason was certainly that the country was one of the very few that had never experienced colonisation. When time came for us to catch the train back to Malaya we called a taxi and directed him to take us to the railway station. We had quite a problem getting him to understand where we wanted to go. When we started out we were not sure he actually knew where we wanted him to take us. As time passed our concern grew. However, we were greatly relieved when we saw, ahead of us, the railway station. We disembarked, paid the taxi driver, and thanked him. We then ran into another problem with the language. Try as we could, we could not make the man in the ticket office understand that we wanted to board the train to Malaya. Fortunately for us someone, who noticed our predicament and could speak a smattering of English, came to our aid. Imagine our shock when he told us that we were at the wrong railway station. There were two railway stations in Bangkok. There was one station for north bound travellers and another for those going south. We were at the one that served the north. We wanted to go south. We quickly found a taxi and at high speed reached the correct station to see the rear carriage of the train, we were hoping to catch, disappearing in the distance. This was Monday and the next train was not due to leave till Thursday. This presented to us with several problems.

We had budgeted very carefully and did not have enough money to stay another three days in Bangkok and also pay for a rail fare home. We also had not booked accommodation. We decided to see if we could get a lift on a freighter going to Penang. We noticed, in the local newspaper, that there was a coal freighter, called the Bratoy, that included Penang in its list of ports of call. We took a taxi to the docks and found the Bratoy tied up at one of the wharfs. We boarded the ship. There was no doubt it was a coal freighter, coal dust was everywhere. There were a few of the crew aboard all wearing dirty sweaty T shirts. One huge seaman approached us, beer in hand, to enquire, in a deep guttural voice, what we wanted. We told him of our predicament. He invited us to join him in a beer and said we were welcome to come aboard and sail with them to Penang. However, after further discussion we found the ship was "open to inducement", meaning that it would go anywhere that a cargo was offered. They would be sailing to Borneo and other places before they reached Penang. This placed us well outside our time limit. We stayed on for a while chatting and drinking and found out that our generous host was the ship's engineer and had, during the war, served as chief engineer on German U Boats. We exchanged histories and by the end of our drinking session had become great buddies and were in total agreement war was stupid.

We left in high spirits and in this state of euphoria, decided that we would spend the rest of our money on a good class hotel and see if we could get a flight back to Penang on Malayan Airways and pay at the other end. The Malayan Airways official was most obliging. He said he would check our credentials with our companies in Penang. He was sure there would be no problem and so booked us on the Thursday flight. Bless his cotton socks.

That evening Maurice and I decided we would go out to a bar cum-restaurant cum-dance hall for a drink and a meal. We were on about our second beer when who should come in but our German ex U-Boat engineer, somewhat the worst for wear. Spotting us he came over and joined us and we were able to repay the hospitality he had extended to us the previous day. Drink eventually got the better of him. He suddenly stood up, and at the top of his voice, started singing Deutchland Deutchland Uber Alles. Not satisfied to sing on his own he "ordered' us to stand up and join him. When we declined he grabbed us by our collars and, to indicate how strong and big he was, easily lifted us both out of our chairs. When we did not sing he demanded we sing. To appease him and prevent the situation getting out of hand we both, for a few minutes, became temporary traitors. Not knowing the words except the title we dah dah and dah-dahed except when we came to the title words that we knew. By that time we were fully into the spirit of the evening and sang the title words we knew with gusto. At the end of this performance, which for a short while made us the center of attraction, he left us to go over to the bar. A few minutes later a scuffle broke out and in another few minutes some small-sized local police came in. A few words were exchanged and they took him away. Fortunately for them he did not resist.

Next day while having breakfast who should come down the hotel stairs to join us but our German friend. He was staying at the same hotel. He apologised for his behaviour on the previous night. He explained that when he left us to go to the bar he got into conversation with one of the people standing there. When he found out the person he was talking to was Norwegian he spat on him. Obviously during the war there was no love lost between the Germans and the Norwegians. Unfortunately the Norwegian turned out to be the Norwegian Consul. Our friend was arrested. As a compromise he was allowed to stay in the hotel that night and was expected, under the auspices of the German consulate, to go to the Norwegian consulate next morning to make an official apology. We both felt sorry for him because at heart he was probably a very generous friendly person.

Thursday arrived and without any undue incident we arrived at the Bangkok Airport. This time the proper airport and the proper 'plane. We boarded our 'plane and commenced our return flight to Penang. We arrived safe and sound and fortunately for us before our leave expired. Malayan Airways kindly allowed us a few months in which to save up and pay the money we owed them.

Back to Work.

The Penang General Hospital.

Not long after returning from leave my friend, Maurice had an accident in a jeep. He was in Penang General Hospital, confined to bed with, for the first few days, his two arms strapped across his chest. At the same time the planter with whom I first shared a bungalow, David B-G, was also in the same hospital suffering from a severe bout of dysentery. He was in the ward next to Maurice. In the same ward, with him, was another assistant, Peter, from our company. Peter had been ambushed on a Dublin Estate road and had been shot in the testicles. He had lost one of them. Little did I know that I would soon join them and actually share the same ward as Maurice.

I was walking through a flooded area of the Estate. I happened to tread on a broken stump of a sapling that was invisible to me as it was under water. This pierced the inside of my left leg from just above the ankle up to my calf. I was immediately transported to the same hospital to join my three friends. It was not long before Maurice and I, in one ward, were moving around in our wheelchairs visiting our two friends in the adjacent ward.

At that time the nursing staff were locals but the Matron was English. She would tolerate no nonsense from anyone. Smoking and drinking were strictly forbidden. But where there is a will there is a way. Our friend Desmond, would visit us and frequently bring with him a business looking case in which were a few bottles of the best. Making sure no one was around Maurice and I would wheel ourselves in to Peter and David's ward, next door, and together the four of us, together with Desmond, would happily consume the contents of the case. We never got caught.

I had been in hospital several days when early one morning Peter called out to us in excitement that he had some good news. We popped into our wheelchairs and went to listen to what he had to say. "Phil", "Maurice" he smiled, last night I had a wet dream, I am OK I am working on one cylinder. We were very happy for him. From then on we nicknamed him Henry Hall. Peter, when he was fully recovered, left Malaya. He returned to England, married and went to Rhodesia as a Tobacco Planter and there, apart from raising tobacco, he raised a family.

David was getting treatment for dysentery. This included being given enemas by a local nurse, behind a movable screen. On one occasion Maurice and I wheeled our chairs up to the screen, stood up, looked over and both of us encouraged the nurse to "stick it in". David was a bit of a prude and told us, in a very prim and proper manner, not to be so rude and go away. The nurse did not seem to mind our intrusion. As you can see we made the most of our stay in hospital.

One very sad event took place some time later. Desmond, for reasons to this day unknown, committed suicide on the estate by shooting himself in the head.

The Crocodile Hunt.

Maurice and I had met up with two Tin Miners, Barney and Tom, who were prospecting for Tin deposits along the Merbau River in north Kedah. Along both sides of the river were dense mangrove swamps. There were a large number of crocodiles in the river and we used to hire a local Malay and his *Sampan* (local open boat) to go shooting them. We did this both day and night but mostly at night because we had very little free time during the day. At night we were able to locate the crocodiles by shining our torches along the river surface. The eye of any crocodile present would glow like the butt of a lighted cigarette. Because of the Emergency, as mentioned before, we were equipped with rifles, sub-machine guns and pistols. Tracers were included in our supply of ammunition. For those not familiar with the word they are bullets that glow in flight so you can see where they are going. We would put about one tracer in five in our submachine guns. They proved a great help when shooting at night. Sometimes we would get a glancing shot at a crocodile and you could hear the bullet ricochet off into the darkness of the night.

The two main hotels in Penang were the E & O (Eastern and Oriental) and the Runnymede. The E & O was the Penang equivalent of the famous Raffles Hotel in Singapore. During the emergency there were a large number of army personnel stationed in Malaya. The Runnymede had been commandeered to house army officers and their wives. Most of the time the wives were left on their own in Penang while their husbands were out patrolling on the mainland. One evening, when we were visiting Penang, Maurice and I dropped in to the Runnymede for a drink. We struck up an acquaintance with two of the wives there. They were very interested to find out that we were planters. They asked us what we did and how we spent our spare time in such an environment. We told them about our social life and also that sometimes we went crocodile shooting. They were very interested in our story about crocodile shooting and thought it must be really thrilling to do something so exciting and adventurous. We said that if they wished we would be pleased to take them on one of our shooting expeditions. They were delighted and jumped at the offer. They said that they would check their husband duty rosters to see when they would be away. They would let us know the date and we could then arrange to come in to Penang to pick them up The appointed day arrived and we set off to Penang Island to pick up our two ladies. We had arranged to meet Barney and Tom at the little fishing village located on the mainland, at the mouth of the Merbau river, about a 2 hour drive north. We arrived there in the early evening. Barney, Tom and the fisherman, with his boat, were waiting there for us. It was a dark moonless night with hardly any wind, ideal for the task in hand. The seven of us carefully boarded the boat. I would have felt a little less apprehensive if it had been a bit bigger. There was not much freeboard to spare. We paddled off slowly into the surrounding dark all sitting upright and motionless. A little further on we started sweeping the surface of the dark slow flowing river with our torch beams looking for the tell-tale red glow. It was not long when one of us shouted out "there's one". The women shouted in excitement. We slowly and silently approached the unsuspecting crocodile and, when we were close enough, fired. We scored a hit. As we paddled towards the croc to retrieve it it started to sink. Barney, obviously not wishing to lose our catch, jumped into the water to retrieve it. The boat rocked precariously and the two women shrieked in fear. I don't blame them. It was their first experience of such a situation. It was pitch dark, they could not truly comprehend what was happening; they were in a strange environment and in fear of capsizing. On top of this, there was Barney, swimming at night in a crocodile infested river attempting to recover our trophy. Things quickly got back to normal when Barney returned to the boat with croc in tow. It was a small croc about 2 meters in length. We took it aboard and laid it in the bottom of the boat. Then carefully, to avoid capsizing, we helped the dripping wet Barney back on board. With our torch lights we lit up our catch. Our two guests were thrilled to have been on a crocodile hunt, at night, upstream in a tropical rain forest river, and were now admiring a real croc lying there in the bottom of the boat, What a wonderful story to tell their friends and family when they returned home.

Unfortunately for them, and us too, this was not the end of the story. The croc was not dead. It was only stunned. Still stunned, and wondering where it was, it started to move. That was the signal for full blown panic. Tom had his pistol in his pocket and started to retrieve it. We shouted to him not to fire till he had pulled it out. In the meantime we started firing on the poor defenseless croc and managed to kill it and end any danger to us. We quickly threw it overboard and were able to relax.

When the sound of the firing died down and we could again concentrate on other things we were brought back to reality not only by the screams of the two women – who would now have a really thrilling and almost unbelievable story to tell - but to our boatman who was shouting at us in a loud voice that his boat and his livelihood were ruined. He was the first to see the results of our shooting. Water was coming up though the floor boards that had been pierced by our bullets. We promised him compensation and told him to Paddle back to his *Kampong* (village) as quickly as possible. In the meantime, with our caps, we plugged the holes in the boat as best as we could and started bailing out the water.

By the time we started on our 2 hour trip back to Penang our two guests had calmed down and it was not long into our return journey that they were chatting about and animatedly recounting the recent events of their once-in-lifetime experience. Unfortunately we never met them again.

Sharing a bungalow.

I had been in charge of the replanting unit since its inception. A newcomer was recruited to take over from me so that I could be posted to Wessyngton Estate in Johor. The new arrival was Ben, who was to share my bungalow. He was a pre war planter and much more sophisticated than I and, as I was to find out later, much better paid. He had a Malay driver who also served as cook, companion and perhaps something else as well? We came to an agreement, that we should divide the bungalow down the middle, using a chalk line and treat each half as our own a distinct abode. The only exception would be the dining table at which we would always share our meals. He insisted that Moktar, and not my Amah, Ah Kim, should do all the cooking because Moktar was a cook par-excellence and he himself was fastidious about food. I was very pleased to agree with his proposal and so was Ah Kim. The first problem arose was the cost of the meals "par-excellence" which I could not afford. I told him that on my salary I could not afford the luxuries he was purchasing. Ben was a generous and understanding person and suggested a flat rate per meal that was well within my means. We settled on that arrangement. The whole idea worked out quite well. It was amusing to invite and be invited across the chalk line for afternoon tea or later on, the drinks. However a more serious problem arose. Ben was a drinker, bordering on being an alcoholic. Before retiring, he would take Benzadrine, to minimize the effects of the drink he had consumed during the evening. The result was that each night he had nightmares. His screams at night, whilst asleep, could be heard throughout the bungalow which was extremely disturbing.

Fortunately, he eventually took over the running of the tractor Unit and I was posted to Wessyngton Estate in central Johor.

Wessyngton Estate.

A First Rate Cook.

The Assistant's bungalow on Wessington estate was only a few hundred feet from the manager's bungalow so security was not a problem. I could therefore, have lived in my own bungalow. However when I arrived on Wessington Estate I was forced to share accommodation with the manager (Davy) as it was impossible, because of the area's bad reputation as a region for terrorists, to get anyone to work there as a cook. We put out feelers but could get no one for the job. Finally one of the Tamil supervisors told us that one of his field gang had told him he had had previous experience as a cook. I immediately arranged to interview him next morning in my own bungalow. Early the next day we met as arranged. He had in tow with him his fat wife who was nursing in her arms a small baby decked out with a woollen knitted hat in all the colours of the rainbow. I thought it only fair, that on his first day, I should give him the easiest of tasks. I said I would be back from the field by about 9:00 for breakfast and told him that for breakfast I would have only bread and a hardboiled egg.

I arrived back at 9.00 a.m. and seated myself at the dining table. The table was bare. Cookie came in and, on the bare table, placed a slice of bread and an egg. His wife with the little baby in her arms kept peering around the kitchen door-screen to see how her beloved was getting along in this most prestigious of jobs; a monstrous promotion from his former employment as a field worker.

I told my new employee that the bread should be on a plate and that the egg should be in an egg cup and that I needed a spoon with which to eat it. These were immediately provided. My newly appointed cook did not depart to the kitchen but hovered behind me to see how I fared. I broke open the top of the egg. I looked inside. It was practically raw! I told him I had asked for a hardboiled egg and this one was soft, in fact raw. His face fell. He picked up the egg, put his finger in it, stirred it around and replied "Ya *Dore* (Tamil for Sir or Tuan) it is soft"

That was the end of his career and also of my chances of moving into my own bungalow. I forthwith moved back into the Manager's bungalow. A few months later I managed to obtain a Chinese cook and at last had a bungalow of my own.

The bungalow was a double story building, which I suppose is a contradiction of the name. One evening when I returned home from an evening at the Kluang Club, I found that in my absence the bungalow had been shot up. No one had been hurt but there were big long gashes where bullets had imbedded themselves in the thick wooden ceiling beams of the ground floor. I had a Ham radio station in my bedroom on the upper floor. I rushed upstairs to see if it had been damaged. I was thankful that everything still worked as normal.

Dedication.

Due to the Emergency the normal five year first tour had been reduced from 5 years to 3 years. So thanks to the emergency instead of working in Malaya for five years I was now going on leave after only 3 years. I was still a junior Assistant on Wessyngton Estate. The Manager, Davy, had been a prewar planter and had, like myself, been a pilot in the Air Force during the war. We became very good friends. Prior to my pending departure on long leave Davy pulled out all the stops to give me a great farewell. There were two other Europeans on the estate at that time. They were the assistant who was to take over from me during my absence, another Maurice, and an ex-Palestine Police Sergeant (Fred) who was in charge of the Malay Special Constables (SCs)..

The four of us sat down in the lounge of the old fashioned bungalow at about five in the evening. The lounge and dining room occupied one very large area. We were provided with whisky, brandy and beer. We drank and chatted till about eight p.m. by which time we were more than slightly under the weather. We then crossed the large floor and sat down at the dining table. In those days the bungalows had huge rooms. The furniture was also large to match the size of the room. The dining table was like a boardroom table. Davy sat at one end facing east where there was a large window. I sat a long way off, at the other end with my back to the window. On my right was Maurice, on my left Fred.

The meal started punctually at eight p.m. Davy had his Indian cook make a complete and sumptuous meal. We started with Hors d'ouvres accompanied by a choice of Brandy, Cointreau, or Crème de Menthe or any combination we desired. None of us were fussy. We chatted spasmodically. The Indian cook would occasionally peep round the kitchen door screen to see how we were getting along with the meal, he had so meticulously prepared for us, and watching to see when he should bring in the next course. Next came soup. In our present mood we took our time so as to fully enjoy the company, conversation and the delicious food served to us. Then, later, came the main course, a wonderful roast with potatoes and vegetables. We did not rush the meal but savoured every morsel. At times I felt as if I was in a trance watching my friends enjoying their drink and food. I am sure they felt the same way. I also noticed that periodically one of them would drop off to sleep.

Before I proceed I must digress a moment to provide a background, for the benefit of those not familiar with the situation on Estates in Malaya during the Emergency. In some of the worst areas in the country, such as the one we were presently in, it was dangerous to go into certain parts of the Estate for fear of being ambushed and killed. As a consequence such places were generally avoided with the consequences that a very troublesome grass, called lallang, would invade the area. If allowed it would grow very densely to waist high, or higher. The communist terrorists were in the habit of setting fire to this grass which would burn fiercely and in doing so damage the rubber trees. Now back to our main course.

We had just finished the main course and Davy was preparing to order the cook to serve up desert when he noticed a red glow through the window facing him. "Good God!" he exclaimed! They've set fire to the lallang in block fortyone. We all turned to look in the same direction and there, no mistaking it was the red glow indication that the communists had set fire to the lallang, which we estimated would be in block fortyone. We were in no fit condition to deal with such a problem. However, to prove my dedication to my job I jumped up, crying out to the others, "We must raise the alarm, and get the labour force out to put out the fire and save the rubber". In one accord we rose and rushed out the front door only to find that the red glow was not as we thought caused by a fire in the rubber – it was sunrise.

My Resignation.

Prior to going on my first long leave, I wrote a letter tendering my resignation. I was frustrated with the old fashioned, restrictive and costly replanting practices. For example the hole into which the new seedling or stump was to be planted had to be exactly 2ft. square and 2 ft foot deep with exactly vertical sides. The assistant was issued with a template to check these measurements. If any hole was even an inch out the worker had to return and carry out cosmetic treatment on the hole until the template fitted. There were dozens of similar wasteful and inefficient practices. To my surprise I was called to Head Office to explain the reasons for handing in my resignation. I mentioned the inefficient practices and stressed that what really concerned me was that not so much the inefficient practices but that no one seemed to have the authority to change them. To my further surprise I was told that if I came back I would be given that authority. I withdrew my resignation. The sequel to this is that about four weeks into my leave I received a letter advising me of an increase in salary – which at that time was extremely welcome. It also was indicative that the promises I had received were likely to be fulfilled.

Australia-my first long leave.

My tour in Malaya should have been five years during which time it was forbidden to marry. *However, because of the Emergency and the tense and dangerous conditions under which we were living, the tour was reduced to 3 years.* At that time my brother was in Sydney and my mother was visiting him. I had intended to go to Australia at the end of my first leave, so the three years instead of five was very fortuitous and timely. Every cloud has a silver lining.

A Temporary Job

One of my objectives in taking a planter's job was to earn enough money to go to Australia and buy a farm. However, this dream was not to be fulfilled. When I left Malaya I was in debt to the Hong Kong and Shanghai Bank to the amount of M$700.00. This may seem a small amount today but in those days it was almost 3 months salary. This might appear to be a most unfortunate situation. I went to see the Bank Manager about this debt. He kindly told me not to worry, have a good leave and that I could repay the debt when I returned from leave. I became a loyal life long customer. *It is an amazing thing how this debt could change my whole life and indeed for the better.*

Leave at that time was for a period of six months. On arriving in Sydney, because I only had $32 to my name, I needed a job in order to pay for accommodation, food and the other necessities of life. My brother had a radio repair business in Sydney. As I was a Radio Ham and my hobby was radio he recommended me as a Radio Mechanic to one of his friends who ran a radio and radio repair shop. There was one other Radio Mechanic in the workshop and a big backlog of radios to be repaired. Obviously there was serious need for my presence. The experience I had, building and repairing my own radio equipment, enabled me to clear up the backlog in very short time. I had an instinct, as did my brother, for diagnosing the problem, and more often than not, without the use of instruments! The backlog vanished on the first day of my employment and I was sitting idle chatting with my co-worker most of the afternoon. This was no way to spend six months leave in summer in Australia with the beach only about half a mile away. So I approached my employer and asked him if he would be agreeable, in view of the speed with which the backlog had been cleared up, for me to take time off from the workshop if there were no more repairs to be done. He knew I was on six months leave from Malaya. I promised I would come in every day and stay as long as there was work to be done. I was pleasantly surprised when he agreed to this proposal. This was Australia. I doubt if such an arrangement would have even been considered in England.

The Boss's Secretary.

A few days after starting employment the boss's secretary, Nina, invited me to partner her in a tennis competition. She thought I was a rich planter and I thought she was a rich farmer's daughter. We were both wrong. I told her that I was not a tennis player. She comforted me by saying she wasn't either. We won the booby prize, a small glass eggcup with the caption "Booby Prize" glued to it. She came from Narromine where the family had a sheep and wheat property. Our friendship eventually resulted in marriage for which I shall be forever grateful.

If I had not been in debt I would not have had to look for a job. If I had not had radio as a hobby I would not have got a job as a radio mechanic in the same shop, where my future wife-to-be was the boss's secretary and I would have missed marrying the most wonderful person I could ever imagine to have as a lifelong companion and of course there would not be the wonderful family which I now have.

I was staying at the Maroubra Hotel on a week to week basis. It had a wonderful location, right on the beach. I had not taken into account that the Christmas holidays would soon be due. A few weeks before Christmas I was told that all the accommodation had been booked for the holiday period. There was no way that my stay there could be extended. Maroubra is a holiday resort and my search for alternative accommodation at that time was unsuccessful. Nina was staying with her mother in a boarding house run by a Mrs. McCarthy. There was a spare room available. Nina approached Mrs McCarthy to see if she would be willing to rent it out to me. Mrs McCarthy was a kindly, elderly woman, who I am sure had a very strong romantic streak in her. I think she sensed a possible romance in the offing. "Bring him along" she said "and if he is as nice as you say he is I will be pleased to have him as a boarder". So a few days later I took up residence there. This was the first of many times that dear Nina helped me out of self-inflicted problems. It amused me that as a consequence, on our marriage certificate, the residence of the bride and of the bridegroom prior to their marriage are the same. That is my story and I am sticking to it.

PART 2

MARRIED LIFE

At the time I asked Nina to accept me in marriage, and she agreed, her mother was at the family farm outside of Narromine. As was the custom in those days, I was expected to formally ask Nina's mother for her daughter's hand in marriage. Narromine was well inland from Sydney so I took an early train which, after a 3 hour journey would arrive there around 9 in the morning. Harold, Nina's elder brother, would meet me at the train station. He ran the farm and this would be our first meeting.

I arrived by train at around 9. a.m. Harold was there to meet me. He introduced himself. He was medium height with fair hair and blue eyes, quite the opposite of his youngest sister. He suggested that, before proceeding to the farm, we should drop into the local pub for a drink, so as to get to know one another a little better, I thought this a very good idea and readily agreed to his suggestion. The pub did not open until 10:00 am. Harold knocked on the door which was opened by the publican, Mick, who immediately recognized Harold. Harold introduced me as his future brother in law and asked if we could pop in for a drink. The publican said it was not opening time yet. Poking his head around the door he looked up and down the street then said come on in. Harold and I hit it off exceptionally well. Conversation flowed easily. We found we had much in common. Time passed swiftly and when at last it dawned on us that should leave for the farm we discovered it was almost closing time. Harold thought it wise to take a peace offering with us. We bought a bottle of plonk (wine to the uninitiated) and some oysters to take back with us which we hoped would placate my waiting future mother-in-law and other relatives patiently waiting, all-day, for our arrival. We arrived at the farm around 10 p.m. Fortunately I was accepted. But if I had not been with Harold I am not so sure the outcome would have been the same.

The visit was the first of many future visits I would make to the farm and to the small farming town of Narromine. It was there that I had my first experience of the farm toilet. It was a small vertical box-like structure, situated quite some distance from the house, complete with a concrete floor and a crude toilet and seat placed over a deep hole dug into the ground. It was of course the good old Australian "Dunny". Old newspapers were available. Placing glossy magazines in the Dunny was taboo.

In the nineteen fifties the same situation existed in the town except that a bucket, and not a hole, was placed under the toilet seat. The Dunny was, for health and other obvious reasons, placed at the end of the garden. Once a week the night soil truck would come and take away the contents and replace the empty bucket. Using the Dunny was not too bad except at night especially if it was raining and of course in winter when it was freezing cold. Getting out of bed in pyjamas and walking with a raincoat over one's head or using an umbrella in the rain was not an experience to be relished. Years later a central sewage system and indoor toilets arrived.

On Saint Valentine's Day, the fourteenth of February, in 1952 Nina and I were married in the Catholic Church in Maroubra, a suburb of Sydney. I did not know it then but I had married the most wonderful, understanding and lovable person that I could only have imagined in my dreams.

Much later, looking back in time, I was able to see the main events that brought me to this happy moment. If I had worn those glasses years ago I would not have got into the Air Force and would probably have remained an academic. If it had not been for the Partition Riots in India I would have become a Tea Planter in India and not a Rubber Planter in Malaya. If it had not been for the emergency in Malaya my tour of duty would not have been cut by two years and I would not have visited Australia at the end of 1951. Because I went on leave in debt I had to get a job. Because I had radio as a hobby I was able to get a job as a radio mechanic where the boss's secretary happened to be the person who was to become my future wife.

Our wedding reception

In anticipation of travelling and residing overseas, in Malaya, Nina had to have vaccinations and inoculations. The inoculations were not a problem but the vaccination was. In Europe it was compulsory for children to be vaccinated for small pox soon after birth. Consequently subsequent vaccinations generally had minimum or no effect. In Australia however, this was not the custom. Nina had never been vaccinated. In order to be vaccinated the required number of days before departure overseas she had to vaccinated no later than two days before our wedding because we would be leaving for Malaya soon after the end of our honeymoon. It was not until a few days into our honeymoon that poor Nina's arm became swollen and inflamed and she was running a high temperature. This was not the ideal situation for either of us to be in on a honeymoon. At least we knew the cause but could do nothing about it until the swelling and temperature subsided naturally.

Married Life in Malaya.

The day came for us to depart. We bade farewell to our friends and relatives and set off to start our married life in a new country. On arrival in Penang Malaya we were met by my bodyguards who handed me my submachinegun and pistol. We then proceeded to the mainland by ferry and then by an armoured car which took us to Dublin Estate about an hour and a half drive. The whole of my adult life had been spent in similar conditions and it never occurred to me that my dear Nina, who had never been out of New South Wales would notice any difference. It is amazing how calmly she took to this massive change in her life. Travelling around in armoured cars with armed bodyguards and sandbags around the walls of our bedroom with armed guards 24 hours a day outside the bungalow. What an amazing person! Many other wives were unable to adapt to the unusual and dangerous situation and they together with their husbands left Malaya.

My first posting on my return from leave was to Dublin Estate where I had started my career. Dublin was the largest of the company's estates. It was also the first estate that I had been posted to when I first arrived in Malaya. It was located in the Bongsu Forest Reserve. We travelled by car to Kulim. From there we transferred to our armoured car which took us to our bungalow on the Estate. There were several communist terrorists (CT) camps in the reserve. So it was too dangerous to live in the isolated Divisional Bungalow.

We were therefore, for security reasons, all accommodated around the" *Padang*" or Common.

When I first arrived in Malaya I was troubled by mosquitoes. I had bites and swellings all over my body and I wondered if I would be able to endure such discomfort during my residence there. Fortunately after a few months I became immune to these mosquito bites. It appeared that I was receiving some sort of inoculation from all the biting I had to put up with and after a time the bites had no affect upon me at all. Nina, on her arrival, experienced the same problem. I was able to comfort her with the knowledge that, hopefully, in a few months' time, she would no longer have to put up with the discomfort of mosquito bites. She never complained.

After our arrival on Dublin Estate we started to raise chickens, ducks and turkeys. We found that for the first month or so of their life the young turkeys needed to be raised in mosquito proof cages. The ducks and chickens did not seem to have this problem. It was probably due to the fact that turkeys were not native to Malaya. As the turkeys grew, they apparently became less susceptible to mosquito bites. Probably like us they had become immunized. We were quite successful with our poultry raising and had plenty of fresh chicken, duck, turkey and eggs on our table.

The Tastiest Bread.

A few small shops were located around the *Padang (common)*. These provided us with the basic essentials. One of these items was delicious tasting bread made by the local baker. Our main essentials were ordered weekly from the Cold Storage on Penang Island and delivered to us by truck.

Nina was interested in doing many of the household chores, including cooking. She asked me if I would find out the recipe and how the local Baker made this delicious bread. She wanted to be able to cook our own freshly made bread. I promised I would look into the matter.

A few days later I remembered my promise and told Nina I would call on the baker early that morning and obtain his recipe. I knocked on the door and was invited in. It was my first visit. He occupied a small wooden hut which, as was common, had shutters instead of windows. There was a planked wooden bed, which the locals customarily slept on without the use of a mattress. There was some basic furniture. The interior was gloomy and humid. There was our fat baker wearing only a sarong, kneading today's consignment of bread on his bed, which for the moment substituted as a table. His bare rolls of flabby flesh were wobbling and dripping with perspiration from the rhythmic effort of kneading the dough. In his mouth was a lighted cigarette. I watched in almost hypnotic amazement as the sweat and cigarette ash rained down and became mixed with the dough. I did not have the fortitude to ask him for his recipe. To be polite I stayed and chatted for a few moments then took my leave. When I arrived home Nina asked if I had found out how the bread was made. I told her "Yes. but you don't want to know." She insisted I tell her which eventually I did. We continued to have the bread delivered. However, a short time later we were making our own bread.

Michelle.

A few months later Nina was pregnant with our first child, Michelle. At that time the army decided to take some action against the CT camps located near by in the surrounding Bongsu jungle reserve. A battery of 25 pounders was set up in front of our bungalow on the *Padang*. Over the next two weeks these fired periodically into areas where suspected CTs were located. I realized, only later, that in view of Nina's delicate condition I should have requested a move to a bungalow located further away from the guns. Men can sometimes appear to be very insensitive.

We were also able to witness, what must have been one of the first attempts, to drop paratroops from the air into jungle. The aircraft and the paratroopers can just be discerned. About five planes came over dropping troops. Subsequent reports, I believe, did not rate the scheme as a success as many troops were caught up in the trees and some suffered minor injuries.

PHOTOS TAKEN FROM OUR BUNGALOW
ON DUBLIN ESTATE.

One of the battery of 25 lb guns
in front of our bungalow

Bombs dropped from aircraft
on suspected nearby CT camps

Paratroopers dropped into
nearby jungle

In early February of 1953, a few months after the shelling and bombing took place, Nina experienced the first symptoms of Michelle's pending arrival. We immediately arranged for the armoured car and for Nina to set out on the two hour journey, which included a ferry trip, to Penang. The Company accountant's wife, who lived in Penang, offered to accommodate Nina. She lived there for a few days before transferring to the Penang General Hospital maternity ward where, on the eleventh of February 1953, Michelle was born. It happened to be Chinese New Year

A week or so later, I, a very proud father, was able to go into Penang and bring both of them back to the estate. Now there were three of us to transfer into the armoured car which took us back to our "home"

Nina and Michelle returning from Hospital
Phil helping Nina and Michelle into armoured car

A few months after Michelle's birth I received my first promotion. I was promoted to Senior Assistant and moved into the bungalow, located in the Head Office area, reserved for the holder of that post. At the same time my mother, who resided in England, visited us.

A Managerial Position. - Wessyngton Estate.

A few months later I received another promotion. I was transferred back to Wessington Estate in central Johor but this time as Manager. I now had an assistant - another Maurice. He and his wife, Esme, also became lifelong friends. About this time all police stations, defense forces, bungalows, and offices on Estates were provided with VHF radios. This gave us a reliable, safe and speedy means of making outside contact. Telephones were not only unreliable but the CTs were continually cutting the telephone lines.

Philip Zeid

The Patrol.

My mother accompanied us to Wessington Estate in Johor from Dublin Estate in Kedah as she still had a few weeks holiday left before returning by ship to England. Wessyngton Estate was located in central Johor, a very bad spot for terrorist activity. Each bungalow had pillboxes around it. These were occupied by armed Special Constables 24 hours a day. A piece of railway line hanging from the roof close to the pillbox was used as a gong. At the manager's bungalow, this was struck each hour on the hour and a response was expected from the other Divisions on the estate to indicate that all was well. As the Estate Divisions were often a mile or more apart, these gongs were given a good hiding and resounded throughout the house. One night before mother's departure a convoy of police vehicles, complete with VHF radios blaring away, arrived at the bungalow around midnight. Our neighbouring police officer, whom we knew very well, entered to advise us that they had word that a group of communist terrorists were reported as crossing our estate and the Police and their Army counterparts had come to seek them out. With all the noise and commotion going on we wondered if we should knock on mother's door and tell her what was happening and that everything was well. We decided against it, thinking that if she was concerned, she would come out herself to find out what was going on. After about an hour and no contact with the CTs, the patrol decided to leave. A little while after they left we heard gunfire. We found out later that the patrol had been ambushed on the way out of the estate. Fortunately no one had been killed. We then went back to bed deciding to discuss what had happened with mother at breakfast in the morning.

Next morning Mother appeared as usual for breakfast. We told her that as she had decided not to come out during all the commotion we decided it was best not to disturb her. Mother's response was "What commotion?" We could hardly believe our ears. She had slept all through the incident. I had forgotten that she was deaf in one ear and must have been lying on the good one throughout the whole affair. We enlightened her on what had happened but I don't think she really took it all in. A few days later when the time came for her to leave we drove her into Singapore and saw her aboard the freighter on which she would be returning to England.

Gunfire – 25 Pounders.

Central Johor was, as already mentioned, an area where terrorists were extremely active. Half way into my first year, as manager, two army officers, accompanied by a battery of 25 pounders, appeared at our bungalow. One of the Officers requested permission to set the guns up near the Estate Office, which incidentally was just at the back of our bungalow. The Estate Office was usually located near the Manager's bungalow. All bungalows were located on a half to an acre of cleared area which was mainly grass lawn with maybe a few flowering bushes or shrubs included. These isolated areas were surrounded by acres and acres of rubber trees. The Officer said that they had information on the possible location of several CT (Communist Terrorist) camps in the surrounding jungle. They would be firing at these locations. He asked if they could set up their tents in our garden and the guns near the office. We were pleased to agree to both requests. That afternoon the officer came over to advise us that they would be firing sporadically from midnight till dawn over the next week. He invited all four of us to join him and the other officer for drinks that evening. At the appointed time we walked the short distance to their tent which they had set up on our lawn, and which served as the "Officers Mess". We arrived at the tent and were warmly welcomed by the two officers in charge. We sat on the ground. There was not enough room for chairs. We men were provided with beer, and very thoughtfully, sherry was available for the ladies. We chatted amicably. As each beer was consumed the empty cans were thrown out through the tent door flap, to provide a timely reminder, in the morning, of how much we had consumed the previous night. Before we realized it, the witching hour of midnight had arrived. The officers reminded us that it was time for them to resume duty. They asked us, ladies included, if we would like to fire a few salvos. We said we would be honoured to do so. We left the tent and walked, maybe staggered I can't remember which, the twenty or thirty yards to where the guns were set up. The gun crews were standing by, guns already aligned on their target. The Officer explained our presence to the sergeant in charge of the guns. Maurice and I were given basic instructions. We took our seats on the gun carriage and held the firing cord. On the instruction "number one gun FIRE" I, being the senior planter present, pulled the firing lanyard of the first gun. There was a resounding bang and flash and the missile shot off into the distant darkness. The gun was immediately reloaded ready for the next shot. "number two gun FIRE" shouted the Sergeant, and Maurice repeated the process with the same result. The firing was repeated down the line. After each firing two or three salvos, there was a pause, and the two ladies were invited to take our place at the guns. Nina looked such a tiny person sitting in the gun seat. At the command "number one gun FIRE" she promptly, and obviously very firmly, pulled the firing lanyard. With a roar another shell shot off towards the distant target. When we had all finished we stood with the two Officers whilst his men continued firing. We eventually thanked them for a very interesting and enjoyable evening and retired to bed. They stayed for a week during which time they showed their consideration by advising us beforehand the time at night they would be firing and for how long. We reciprocated their hospitality by each of us inviting them to dinner.

We were all very pleased to have had the opportunity of throwing a greater weight of ammunition at the CTs than they could ever hope to throw at us. We do not know the results achieved by this operation. However, as it was certain there were camps in the area, the salvos, at the very least, would give the CTs a few worrisome and sleepless nights.

The Arrival of our second child – Margaret.

The time came for Maurice and his family to go on Long Leave. This was about the time that Nina was expecting our second child to be born. Before departing on their overseas trip all three of them needed to be vaccinated and inoculated and their health certificate endorsed accordingly. The only hospital in the area was the British Military Hospital (BMH) in Kluang, about 30 miles away. We only had one armoured car on the estate. It was therefore customary, if one of us was to go off the estate, to notify the other so that he would know where the armoured car was. Maurice had made arrangements for he, his wife Esme and their son Stephen to be inoculated and vaccinated at the BMH on the afternoon 25th of October 1954. Maurice approached me for use of the armoured car which was granted.

No sooner had I returned to the bungalow when Nina told me that Margaret, who had been cooped up for nine months, thought she had enough and decided she wanted out. I rushed to the assistant's bungalow hoping to catch Maurice before they left so that we could all go to the hospital together in the armoured car. They had already left. I called my driver; we got into our unprotected car and drove off to Kluang. Half way there we came across the armoured car. It had been ambushed and fired on and gone into the ditch. The CTs did not follow up on the attack but withdrew. No one was harmed. The Malay SCs said they would be able to manage on their own and suggested we take their three passengers with us. We drove off to the British Military Hospital in Kluang. The nurses were surprised to see us as this was the first time they were made aware that there was a pregnant European woman in the area. Our local doctor, who visited the Estate once a week, to check on the health of the workforce did not handle Pregnancies. Also the local paramedic (known as a Dresser), never handled maternity cases either nor saw pregnant women. Pregnancies and births among the Tamil workers on the estate were handled by their own midwives. The nurses told us that none of them had ever delivered a baby before but not to worry. A little later the armoured car arrived and Maurice sent Esme and Steven, their young son, back to the estate. He and I then went to the White Horse Hotel in Kluang for a drink and to periodically phone the hospital to find out how things were going. Margaret was born that evening. She was a chubby healthy looking child. Maurice and I who had already celebrated the anticipated arrival of my second child visited Nina and our new born, Margaret, and then proceeded back to the estate.

The next morning Esme, Maurice's wife, arrived at the BMH to visit Nina and see our new born daughter. She parked her car close by. A short while after her arrival, and whilst they were chatting together, the Colonel of the unit entered the room. He was obviously peeved to find Esme's car parked in a non-parking area. She had done so in ignorance of the rules on the base. He gruffly told them that planters' wives seemed to think they could park anywhere and not obey the normal rules that others were subject to. The two women had been subject to years of stress and of living under very arduous and dangerous conditions. The last 24 hours had not been a tea party. His comments and their timing was the trigger that released their long pent up emotions. From deep down there welled up, in both of them, an uncontrollable force. They both spontaneously, and without really knowing why, burst out sobbing, tears streamed down their faces and their behaviour was almost bordering on hysteria. There was nothing that could stop them. The poor Colonel was taken aback, shocked and highly embarrassed. He was helpless to do anything. He had no alternative but to leave.

Nina told me, later, when they had calmed down that they were both at a loss to explain why they had simultaneously broken down. They felt embarrassed and sorry for the poor Colonel. Later that afternoon the Colonel returned, presented Nina with a bunch of flowers and apologized for his behavior that morning. Nina gracefully accepted the flowers and also apologized for her and Esme's inexplicable and unintended loss of control earlier that morning. They parted good friends.

Margaret eventually returned home to Wessington Estate and Michelle, her older sister, now had a companion. Unfortunately Margaret did not thrive as expected. She could not keep her food down. Several trips to the hospital were made to see if they could determine the cause. Unfortunately no one there had the necessary experience with babies to recommend what should be done. We were told to increase the strength of her milk but this did not help. Probably it would have been better to have diluted it but we were not to know. Many sleepless nights followed with Margaret crying throughout most of them. The poor little thing was in great distress. It was almost four months before she regained birth weight and started to improve.

White Ant Treatment.

Inspection of the Estate buildings for white ants and their eradication had been neglected throughout the war years. It was only several years after the reoccupation of our Estates in Johor, that a company treating white ants was established in Singapore. The proprietors were a newly arrived Australian father and son team. I phoned them and made an appointment. The son would arrive at 8:00 a.m. which for him meant a very early start. On his arrival we went straight to work. I showed him one building after another that required inspection and possibly treatment. He soon impressed me as a very knowledgeable person. As we moved from building to building he identified, immediately, shot-hole borers, pinhole borers, dry rot and physiofolis borers. (I hope I have the spelling right) which were the ones that made one inch diameter holes in the roof timbers.

We then came to my old wooden bungalow, the one I had occupied on my previous tour when I was a bachelor. It was a double story wooden building with a solid timber ceiling which also served as the floor of the upper part of the house. He studied the holes in the ceiling and was unable to make a quick diagnosis, as he had when visiting the previous buildings. "To save you embarrassment", I said, "They are bullet holes."Bullet holes!" He exclaimed "Why would there be bullet holes in the ceiling?" It was then that I realized he could not be aware of the "Emergency" on the mainland. To me this was unusual but it could have been that he was newly arrived and also was living in Singapore to which the emergency had not spread. I explained briefly the situation.

Planters start their working day before sun-up and return to the bungalow for breakfast later in the morning. As my old bungalow was the last on the list for inspection, and it was now my normal breakfast time, I asked him if he would like to join me and my family for breakfast. He accepted with pleasure. We arrived at my bungalow to find our local visiting European doctor, sitting there in shorts and a T shirt, unshaven, with a glass of brandy in his hand talking to Nina. I introduced my visitor who, I said, would be joining us for breakfast. Our doctor was normally very well groomed and smartly dressed. In view of his unusual condition and appearance I asked him what the hell had happened?

"Phil" he replied" "I have been up all night. I got a call on the VHF from Layang Layang (our neighbouring Estate) that CTs (Communist Terorists) had come into the local Chinese shop and demanded money and food from the proprietor. The wife started screaming. The CTs shot the shopkeeper and slit the wife's throat. They told me that the wife was still alive and asked me to get over as quickly as possible. When I got there, blood was pouring out of the cut in her neck. I fixed her up as best as I could and came on over here. I'm pretty sure she will live". Our guest listened to all this in silence. When it was all over he looked at his watch and said he had just remembered he had an urgent appointment in Singapore. He apologized for not accepting our offer of breakfast and promptly left. We never received a quote and also never saw him again.

Bristol Estate.

My next transfer was as manager of Bristol Estate. Bristol Estate was situated in the Selangor in central west Malaya. It was just before Christmas when I developed a very high temperature and became delirious. I was immediately transferred to the general hospital in Kuala Lumpur. As on previous occasions, I was already on the way to recovery. I recall the hospital being in a very dilapidated condition. When I became fully aware of my surroundings I noticed buckets strategically placed on the floor to catch the rain water leaking through the roof. Much later, the hospital was repaired and became a first class hospital. During my stay in hospital the assistant who had been my assistant on Wessyngton Estate also, for security reasons, kindly moved into the bungalow with Nina and family to look after them in case of an emergency. It was not long before I was fighting fit and back to work again.

Louis.

It was while we were on Bristol Estate that Louis arrived. It was in the same hospital, in Kuala Lumpur, where I had been sick where he was delivered. Everything went very smoothly and now we had a family of three lovely children.

A Dinner for our Chinese and Indian friends.

We had become close friends with the young Chinese contractor on the Estate as well as the Indian District Officer and his wife who were located about one hour's drive north of the estate. We thought it would be nice to invite them both, together with their wives, to an early evening curry. The first to arrive was the young Chinese contractor, who, probably not knowing European custom had brought along four of his friends. This was quite unexpected, but as we always over-catered, it did not present a problem. We welcomed them all in a very friendly fashion. We told them that we were expecting another couple and hoped they didn't mind waiting. As waiting meant more drinking there was no objection to the idea. It was beginning to get rather late and our guest mentioned that they hoped they would not have to wait much longer because they had a late rendezvous with friends in Kuala Lumpur that night for a gambling session. In view of the circumstances we decided to start the meal and hoped that when our other guests arrived they would understand the circumstances under which we had started without them. We were about half way through the meal and they had still not arrived – most unusual. I thought maybe they had the wrong date and that I should phone them to check. Imagine my amazement when on contacting them they said "Thank Goodness you phoned". We knew we were invited to a curry this evening but we could not remember who invited us. Forgive us Phil but we have been sitting here all dressed up ready to leave immediately. I told them it was very late and they had an hour to drive to get here and I and Nina would understand if they would prefer to join us another time. "Not at all" he replied we are on our way.

I went back and told Nina what had happened and that she could expect our second lot of guests to arrive in about an hour. We had time to complete our meal and bid farewell to our Chinese friends who were returning to Kuala Lumpur. The table had been cleared and reset when our second lot of guests arrived. We did not tell them that we had already eaten with other friends but sat down to start a second meal, to which we did not and could not do justice. The evening went very well but continued to very late. We eventually bade farewell to our friends and retired to bed after a very unusual evening of entertaining.

Back to North Malaya - Harvard Estate.

In 1956 I was posted to Harvard Estate as Manager. The company's two largest estates were Dublin and Harvard both located in the Malay state of Kedah. These two Estates were considered the senior Estates and to become manager of one of them gave one considerable prestige in the company and the district. On arrival on the Estate we found that the manager's bungalow was in the final process of being renovated. An assistant's bungalow close by was empty and so Nina and I with our family decided to move into it rather than put up with the inconvenience of having work done on the house while we lived in it. Many of the Executive Staff in the area could not understand how a Senior Manager on the largest estate in the area would choose to live in an Assistant's bungalow, instead of the more prestigious Manager's bungalow, in spite of the inconvenience involved.

Harvard estate was unique. It had a very large factory which made centrifuged and creamed latex. The creamed latex plant was, I believe, the largest, if not the only one in the country. The executive staff on the estate were from UK and were planters. The executives operating the factory were also from UK but were technicians. There was also a research group who were all Americans, who incidentally were all on a higher salary scale than the other two groups. For some reason, lost in the distant past, these three groups did not mix with one another and rarely, if ever, inter- socialized, yet they all lived together in one large compound close to the estate Head Office.

We very soon became aware of this unsatisfactory situation. We had only been on the Estate less than two weeks when Nina decided it was time to throw a really big party and get the three dissenting groups together.

We had invented a cocktail that worked as a real party starter. We had tried many other alcoholic mixtures but none worked as good as what we called our beloved "Between the Sheets". Some of the cocktails that we had previously tried, made people tired, others made them disagreeable, but our special cocktail seemed to give guests a new lease on life together with stamina to continue partying into the early hours of the morning - as a long as they did not consume too much.

The secret ingredients were; Bacardi Rum, Brandy, Cointreau and a special concentrated sweet lemonade. However, to have the full and desired effect the proportions had to be exactly right and the method of serving strictly adhered to. The mixing and preparation itself was a really enjoyable task and something to look forward to as, during its preparation, it required continuous sampling to ensure the proportions were correct. This meant you had to have plenty of time and no other commitment for the rest of the day. You started off by adding equal quantities of Bacardi and Brandy, the total quantity being dependent on the number of guests you were inviting. The next step was to add the Cointreau very slowly, stirring it in and sipping small samples until you could just detect the orange flavour of the Cointreau. If you overshot the mark you added a little more Bacardi and Brandy. You were now ready to add the concentrated sweet lemonade. This you added slowly until you could not distinguish between the orange and lemon flavour. If you added too much sweet concentrated lemonade then you had to add more rum and brandy and Cointreau to compensate. The object was to achieve the right blend so that when you tasted the final mix you could not tell whether the dominant taste was orange or lemon. The sweetness of the lemonade concentrate had the effect of disguising the underlying high alcoholic content of this very potent mixture and making the drink appear to be very innocuous. However, there was still another and most important step which took place before the drinks were served. The mixture was poured into bottles and stored in the freezing compartment of the refrigerator. Because of the high alcoholic content it never froze so we never had to worry about the bottles breaking in the fridge. Small glasses, which had also been stored in the freezing compartment, were used to serve the drinks. This was to prevent the drink warming up, before being completely consumed, which was more likely to happen if the serving glasses were bigger. The drink was served as guests arrived. It was such an apparently innocuous drink that we often had competitions to see if our guests could guess what the contents were. Many of them often said it was a fruit squash with perhaps a little alcohol added.

This is what we used as a starter at our first party on Harvard Estate to which we invited all three groups. As you will see from the results it is very advisable indeed, to limit the number of such drinks served per person.

One by one the guests arrived and each was served with a small ice cold glass of our special mixture taken directly from the freezer. It was not long before all our guests had arrived and had been served no more than two of our special drinks, which we knew from experience, was a suitable and safe limit. The drinks had worked their magic and partying was in full swing. Our guests were now being offered drinks of their own choice. It was very unusual but one of our planters was a German. He told us that our special drink was nothing unusual and asked for more. We explained the situation to him and declined to offer him another glass of our special mix. A short time later our German friend approached us, with one of our special mixes in his hand, saying there was nothing special to our drink. On completion of this statement, his body seemed to stiffen and then he proceeded to fall backwards. Fortunately the room was crowded enough for him to not fall backward onto the ground with consequent personal injury. He was completely unconscious not from any physical injury but from the drink. We tried to revive him but all our attempts were futile. There was nothing we could do except to load him into one of our cars, take him back to his nearby bungalow, and put him to bed. On returning I went into the kitchen to ask our servants how our friend had got hold of more of our special drink. They told me he had come into the kitchen and in spite of their objections, had helped himself to more of our special drink, which we kept in the freezer. The party continued till dawn when a bacon and egg breakfast was served. Then everyone departed as the best of friends and vowing to keep up a friendly relationship in the future. Later that day we heard that our engineer, on his way back home, had driven his car into a ditch but fortunately with no damage to himself, his passengers or his car. And so ended a wonderful and very exceptional party.

Moving to Head Office, Penang Island.

One of the special positions in our Head Office was that of "Inspector". The inspector's job was to periodically visit all the Estates and see that all procedures were properly carried out and that the Estate was being run in a satisfactory manner. Most other Plantations employed an Agency to manage the running of their estate and assess their progress. These Agencies carried out this work, for a fee, using what were known as 'Visiting Agents'. The job was the same. It was decided, by Head Office, that the Inspector needed an assistant. I was fortunate to be selected to fill this post and very shortly afterwards my family and I moved in to a house on Penang Island. Remembering my resignation at the end of my first tour, because of the inefficiency that was occurring within the organisation, here was I now able to make some real changes. Very fortunately, the Inspector was a tolerant and understanding person with whom I got on very well. Our company's Operational Manual allowed for no diversion from the instructions that it contained, even if those instructions were outdated and inefficient. I suggested to my superior that the manual should be rewritten and he agreed. Another matter of great concern to me was the numerous forms that had to be filled up monthly which contained no information relevant to our current operation. They were pre-war forms which may have had a use at that time. I asked for permission to review the use of all forms submitted to Head Office and determine if they had any real use. If not they would be eliminated and if they contained useful information the contents would be reviewed to determine if they needed modification to bring them up-to-date or simplified. Again my proposal was accepted.

In rewriting the manual I wished to make it clear that it was a guide containing what were considered to be the best current practices but that these practices could be changed if sufficient evidence was provided to show that the change would be more beneficial than the current procedure. To stress this the opening page of my new manual started with the statement : – "The operating instructions and suggestions in this manual are considered to be the best available practices at the current time. However, if anyone discovers what they consider to be a better practice or method please submit your reasons, and results if any, for making a change. Such proposals will be welcome as we wish at all times to improve the company procedures."

The matter of excessive paperwork was speedily dealt with. The first thing I did was to list all forms that I thought had no useful purpose. I then sent this list as an internal Memo to all staff in the office, asking who had use for this information and if so what they did with it. Not surprisingly, many of the forms were never used. These were the ones that I intended to eliminate. However, I still had a problem to resolve before I could write to the estates and tell them to cease compiling this useless information and sending it to Head Office. Many of the Head Office staff were concerned that we might need this information in the future and as we had been compiling it for many years we would be losing valuable information and the continuity of recording this information would be lost. The fact that we had been compiling thjis information pre-war and also for 10 years post-war and no one had ever had use for it seemed to make no difference. Finally logic prevailed and I was able to advise all Estate Managers that these irrelevant forms need no longer be submitted.

Replacement of the Tractors used in Replanting.

The manufacturers manual on tractors recommended replacement after 20,000 hours of use or 10 years whichever came first. The time had arrived for replacement of the tractors. This was going to be a very costly operation. Our American Vice President in charge of Plantations came out to discuss this matter with those involved. I nor the personnel in charge of replanting units on the Estates were included in the meeting! My boss, the Inspector, was one of the participants. The meeting went on for a considerable time. The decision was finally made to replace all tractors at a cost of several million dollars. The next day the Vice President flew back to America. When I heard of the decision I immediately pointed out, that regardless of what the manual said about the replacement time, the tractors were good for many more years to come. I backed this up by pointing out that the only things that wore out were the large rear sprocket wheel, the chain tracks and track pins and the front idler over which the chain track ran. These we built-up by welding and we had reused them in this way several times. When no more build-ups could be done new items were purchased to replace the worn out ones. The only other item of concern was the diesel engine which drove the tractor. This again only needed good and regular maintenance to keep it running for many more years to come. To prove my point I produced the records that I had kept over the years that I was in charge of the replanting unit. The Inspector was impressed and also convinced that we did not need to replace out fleet of tractors. A quick meeting was convened with, this time, myself included, to convince and obtain agreement from the other parties that we should continue to use the tractors that we had and that we should cancel the planned purchase of new equipment. Agreement was reached and a telegram was immediately sent to the VP telling him that we had changed our plans. We would continue to use our present fleet of tractors and that we would no longer be purchasing new ones. An explanatory letter would follow. The VP replied immediately asking how it was possible that after such a long deliberation which concluded with a unanimous decision to replace the whole fleet, that within one day of making that decision it had been reversed ? Someone else, not me, would have to provide the explanation. We continued to use the same tractors for another eight years until all replanting was completed at which time they were all sold in good running condition.

Eventually the Inspector, with whom I had become very good friends, passed away from illness and I was promoted from assistant inspector to Inspector.

We had a sister company in Sumatra which pre-war had administered the properties in Malaya through the Malayan Head Office. The post-war situation in Indonesia was rather precarious and probably, as a consequence, we now operated independently from our sister company in Sumatra. In fact I was called on to periodically inspect the Indonesian Company. Other than the General Manager, who was American, most of the executive staff were Dutch with a few Indonesians. All the staff were very cooperative and a pleasure to work with. On each visit I would stay in the General Manager's bungalow. I became very good friends with him and his wife. On occasions I would visit with my wife and we would enjoy some local Indonesian food especially prepared for her visit. Eventually the General Manager of our Malayan operation was promoted to Vice President and moved to our American Head Office. I was chosen to replace him as General Manager.

Patricia and John.

It was whilst residing in Penang and almost 10 years after our first child, Michelle, was born, that Patricia arrived. Patricia's delivery was very complicated and difficult but all ended well and both mother and daughter left the Penang General Hospital in good health.

John's arrival three years later, was very interesting. We were playing bridge with friends when at about midnight Nina realised that John was about to arrive. We rushed off to the 7th Day Adventist hospital Penang where a few hours later

John arrived. I was notified of this event and quickly went to see our new son. When I picked him up I was startled to see that the soles of his feet were purple. Nina had not noticed this before. We were very worried. We immediately called the nurse who explained that it was their practice to provide new parents with footprints of their latest child. The purple colour was the ink.

John's footprints 1 day old

We now had a wonderful family of five children, three girls and two boys.

Our Travels in Europe.

On one of our six month leaves to England, when our three older children were five years of age and under, we hired a Fiat 1100 and took them on a four months tour of France, Italy, Holland, Belgium, Germany and Liechtenstein. Eight years later we did the same again with a larger family and the added luxury of living in a motor camper. This time, in addition to visiting the same countries as on our previous holiday, we also included a visit to Lourdes and also tours of England, Scotland and Wales. The happy times we had together would provide material for another book

General Manager.

Our General Manager was transferred to our New York office to become Vice President and I was chosen to replace him. I seemed to settle into this job without much problem. I had built up a good and close relationship with all staff from the office boy to the Accountant. My door was always open and anyone was welcome to drop in at any time. Early in my career this resulted in a very interesting incident occurring.

At the time this incident occurred Asian staff were not employed as Executive Staff on any of the foreign owned Plantations in Malaya. Some were however employed in Head Offices' as, maybe, accountants. The highest ranking local staff members on the estates were clerks or supervisors. Our Company was one of the first, if not the first, to take steps to change this situation. Two of our brightest field supervisors, known as Conductors, were selected for special promotion. They were Ramasamy and Dorasamy (not their real names).

Those that introduced the scheme thought it prudent to proceed gradually. Therefore as a first step a new intermediate rank was created between that of Conductor and Assistant. These two gentlemen were put on special increased salaries; they were given more authority than customary. They were provided with a bungalow equivalent to that of an executive of Assistant rank a car and certain other executive privileges.

The time eventually arrived for Dorasamy to retire. He was given a party and a great send-off. He was presented with the usual watch that everyone, no matter what their status in the company, received on their retirement.

Several months had passed since his departure when I received a letter from our Head Office, which was located in the USA. Dorasamy had complained that he had been badly treated, underpaid and that his retirement payment was meagre and insufficient for him to survive. In addition in recognition of his excellent long and loyal service to the company he had received nothing but a cheap watch. He was asking Head Office for an ex-gratia payment to help overcome the difficult financial situation in which he found himself and to compensate for the poor treatment he had suffered during his employment. I was asked to explain.

I prepared my reply. I pointed out that he was one of two of the most favoured staff. I provided the salary he received compared with others and also provided his retirement payment, which was quite considerable. I also pointed out that he had had more privileges than all other staff, except one other who was in a similar situation to him. I also mentioned that the watch he received on retirement was the same as I would receive when I retired. I never heard any more about the matter from Head Office, so I presumed that they were satisfied with my explanation.

However, this was not the end of the story. A few months later Dorasamy appeared at my door. I invited him in. I am sure he did not know that I knew of his complaint to Head Office. I greeted him in my usual friendly fashion and asked after his family and how life in retirement was going. For a while we discussed matters in general and then he came to the point of his visit. He asked me if, in view of his long loyal service, the company could give him some more money. I asked him why? He replied he had been underpaid. I pointed out that, in his work capacity, he was one of the two highest paid people on the staff list. He stated that he could have received a much higher salary if he had moved to another company. I told him that in that case he should have done so. He then said that he had received a very meagre retirement benefit. I was able to tell him the approximate amount he had received, which was quite considerable. He then complained about the watch he had received. I told him that that was the standard watch that everyone received, in fact I would receive the same watch on my retirement. For a while we both sat in silence. We were getting nowhere. Then suddenly Dorasamy came up with what he thought was a brilliant idea.

He told me that we had in our budget a sum of M$72.00 per year per person to cover sickness and hospitalisation of staff. He had worked for 32 years without once being sick. This amounted to M$2,304.00 which the company had not spent on him. So surely he was due this amount. I pointed out that the $72.00 was not the same all the years he had worked. Years ago the amount was much less. Also this amount was an average that in total was budgeted to cover the small percentage of those who actually became sick. It was not meant to be an individual entitlement. Whilst talking I saw a way out of this dilemma. So I said. "Even so if I give you this money will it satisfy you? And if so will you promise never to bother me again with this matter nor make any more claims." With a great smile he agreed. He had won the day.

I called for Wong our accountant and told him to make out a cheque to Dorasamy for $2304.00 and to book it as "A refund for his never being sick during his 32 years of employment." Wong left the room obviously puzzled and shortly returned with the cheque which he handed to me and promptly left the room. Dorasamy rose from his seat and leaned over expecting me to pass him the cheque. "Just a moment Dorasamy" I said. Before I hand you this cheque I have a few words to say "God has been good to you Dorasamy" I said. "He has given you 32 years of good health. Now in return you are telling him that all your years of good health is only worth M$2,304.00" I prepared to hand the cheque over to him. Then I added "so if as you pass through the door with this cheque in your hand you suffer a heart attack don't blame me. "Here is the cheque. I said, handing it to him. Suddenly with a strange look on his face, he withdrew his hand and still facing me, he backed away. Then, without a word, he moved to the door. As he passed through the door he placed his hand on his heart and moved out of sight.

I called Wong, handed him the cheque and told him to cancel it. I never heard from Dorasamy again.

I would not have done this if Dorasamy were a Chinese. He would have taken the money, gone down to the local temple and offered up, as a burnt offering, tenfold the amount or so, in "temple-money" in thanksgiving to his god. At that time I doubt if a Malay would have stooped to the point of making such a request.

Confrontation between Malaya and Indonmesia.

It was just after the Confrontation period with Indonesia when I was asked to inspect our sister Company's property in Sumatra for damage that might have been done during our absence, when the Indonesians had taken over our Estate. At that time the airport, which is located on Penang Island, was under repair and aircraft servicing Penang were using the RAAF landing strip located at Butterworth. To take the aircraft from Penang to Medan included making a trip by ferry from Penang to Butterworth took some considerable time.

Most of the flights I took were local and did not require a passport or a health certificate. On this occasion, probably because I was going to the mainland, I forgot that I was going overseas and set out without my passport or health certificate. It was only on arrival at Butterworth airport that I realised I had left without these two important documents. I immediately phoned my wife on Penang Island and said I was sending my driver, Ali, back to collect these two important documents. If the airport had still been on Penang Island, the trip would not have taken very long, but being on the mainland meant it would be unlikely that I would have the documents before the plane was due to take off. This in fact proved to be the case. While I was still waiting for Ali to arrive the passengers were called to board the plane. By chance I saw the pilot about to board and recognised him as Nick, one of the pilots with whom I had become very friendly. I explained the situation to him. He was very sympathetic. He told me that he that he had authority to delay the departure of the aircraft for up to 15 minutes after which he would have to contact Head Office and provide a very good reason for any further delay. There was no good reason and so my time was limited to another fifteen minutes. The fifteen minutes were up and Ali had still not arrived. I was informed that the aircraft was about to take off. I asked if my baggage could be taken off and was told it was not possible but that they would return it on the next flight. At that moment Ali arrived. He handed me the documents. The officials processed them quickly and pointed out that my health certificate did not include an up-to-date smallpox vaccination which at that time was essential for entry into Indonesia. At the time, if you wished to enter Malaya or Indonesia it was necessary to be vaccinated for smallpox and have proof of vaccination on the Health Certificate. I said I was willing to take a chance of arriving in Medan without an up-to-date vaccination. They said it would be up to the captain of the aircraft to decide if, under those circumstances, he would take me because if the authorities in Medan refused me entry, he would have to bring me back. I said I was prepared to take that chance and hurriedly ran across the tarmac and boarded the aircraft. I explained the situation to Nick who, with all the passengers, had been waiting in a boiling hot aircraft, sweltering in the heat and wondering why they had not taken off yet. Nick in exasperation and to prevent any further delay said "for heavens sake Phil get seated" and prepared to take off.

The short trip was uneventful and we eventually landed at Medan. I decided the best thing to do was to produce my passport but not present my Health Certificate in the hope it would not be asked for. I had travelled to Medan on many occasions and always handed both documents in for inspection so I did not know what to expect on this occasion.

I was quite surprised and very relieved when I passed through immigration without being asked for my Health Certificate. I proceeded to customs which was the only barrier remaining between me and my friend "Sunny" who was waiting to pick me up and take me to the rubber estate.

There were eight managers on the Estate I was visiting and I had bought eight digital watches, one for each of them, as a present or *oleh oleh* as such gifts were customarily called. The customs officer opened my bag and eyed the eight watches, which I had previously declared. In those days Indonesian officials were often out to get whatever they could. Then he said to me have you got one of these for me? If I had said no there was every possibility that I would have had problems with the Customs Department for bringing in so many watches. In my, at that time, minimal Indonesian, I told him that he was welcome to take one but that as there were eight managers on the Estate I would only be able to give seven of them a watch and I would be very ashamed that I could not give the eighth person a watch also. The Indonesians and Malays are inherently very polite people and would not dream of causing embarrassment to anyone. So without hesitation he refused my offer, shut the bag, marketed it as having been inspected and wished me a pleasant stay

My first action on arriving on the Estate and having settled into my accommodation was to visit the Estate doctor in order to be vaccinated for smallpox. I was under no illusion that I could re-enter Malaya without having an-up-to date smallpox entry in my health certificate. I might have been extremely fortunate once but it was outside the realms of possibility for this to happen a second time, especially entering Malaya. The doctor was a large French Canadian, who spoke with a pronounced French accent. We greeted one another and after a short discussion I told him that I had arrived without a smallpox vaccination and that I had not handed in my health certificate on arrival and fortunately had not been asked for it. I had come for a smallpox vaccination because I would not be able to return without one. "Phil" he said, in his strong French accent "I have zee fresh vaccine but when I used it on my last two patients zeir arms 'blew' up. " I am very worried. I am sure the vaccine is contaminated and I dare not use it. It is dangerous. I have ordered more but it will be a month or so before it arrives. So I am afraid I am unable to give you a vaccination". "Doctor" I said "if I cannot be vaccinated, would you perhaps be able to sign my Health Certificate? If not, I do not think I will be able to return to Malaya until your vaccine arrives?" To my delight and surprise he replied "of courze"; and my problem was solved. I completed my inspection in just under two weeks and was pleased to find that the Estate was in fairly good condition. I think this was primarily due to the fact that the current staff had been left to carry out their duties.

The Malayan Emergency.

The terrorist insurgency in Malaya was known as The "Emergency". It lasted from 1948 to 1958. Malaya did not become known as Malaysia till July 1st 1957 when it ganed it's independence. The emergency was a serious matter. Many local people were killed as were many planters and tin miners. There were many train derailments. Sir Henry Gurney, The High Commissioner to Malaya, was ambushed and killed by members of the Malayan Communist Party.

(MCP) on his way to Fraser's Hill. It was believed that this was more a coincidence than a planned ambush. The Malayan Army, Malay Special Constables, troops from England and Australia and the Commonwealth were all involved, yet the overall operation was a Police Operation and remained under the police and the civilian government's control. Compared with situations in Korea, Vietnam and especially Iraq and Afghanistan and other trouble spots throughout the world, the Malayan situation had everything going for it. Even so it lasted 10 years! What were these important differences? I will explain.

The people mostly intimidated by the Chinese communist terrorists were the rural Chinese and other non-Malay inhabitants – these were mostly Indian. The former mainly lived in small isolated smallholdings raising pigs, chickens, and growing vegetables. They did not own their smallholdings but were mainly squatting on government land. They also lived in the villages where they were generally shopkeepers. They were ideal targets for the communist terrorists who needed food and money. They were consistently intimidated and forced to provide these items.

The rural Malays lived under similar conditions as the Chinese except they owned their land. They also farmed, mainly producing rice. Some also lived in the villages together with the Chinese. It would be thought that during the Emergency they would also have been intimidated and threatened by the terrorist. However, except for a few incidents at the beginning of the Emergency, they were never touched. The reason is very simple and obvious.

During the early days of the Emergency a couple of Chinese terrorists came across some Malays hunting in the jungle. At that time not everyone realised that the terrorist organisation was well spread throughout the country. The two Malay hunters were therefore quite surprised when the Chinese held them up and took their rifles away from them. To have this done to them, especially by Chinese, who in general they had no time for, incensed them to such an extent that their anger knew no bounds. They ran Amock, pulled out their *parangs*, (a large broad-bladed knife used by Malays) and beheaded the Chinese on the spot. Incidentally the word "Amock" derives from the Malay word which describes this unique Malay behaviour. About the same time some Chinese terrorists entered the village of Bukit Selambau, in the northern state of Kedah, about ten miles from the estate I was currently on. A group of Chinese communist came into the village, whose occupants were mostly Chinese, and threatened the villagers with death unless they gave them food and money. In the process a retired former Malay policeman was killed. Three or four days later Malays from the surrounding villages and rice fields came into the town and killed almost every Chinese man, woman and child in the village. After these and perhaps a few more similar unknown isolated incidents, the Malays, throughout the whole ten years of the Emergency, were never ever troubled again by the Chinese communists.

Winning the Hearts and Minds.

One of the main objectives of government, as part of the scheme to combat the Communist Terrorists, was to improve the livelihood and safety of as many people as possible, especially those living in rural areas. The local cattle were skinny creatures and delivered little milk. In an effort to quickly improve the livestock all bulls throughout the country were rounded up and castrated. High pedigree Sindhi Bulls were brought in from India and located strategically throughout the country. The locals would bring their cows to these locations for insemination. In a few years the quality of the livestock improved dramatically and even a dairy industry started to evolve.

A similar program took place in the country villages, known as *Kampongs*. The best farmers in each Kampong were interviewed. They were told that they had been selected because of their skills in raising poultry. They would be given two pairs of pedigree chickens to raise. These were to be kept separately in order to produce a separate and new flock of birds. They were told that the quality of their stock would improve and so would their egg yield. All that was required in return was that, once they had sufficient of their new stock, they were to return two or more pairs of birds to make up for what was given to them.

By the time they were in a position to do this their neighbours had become envious of the improved birds that their friends were rearing and wanted some also. There were now several sets of quality birds available and these were given to other farmers, with the same conditions applying. The availability of pedigree birds increased exponentially. It was not long before there was a marked improvement in the poultry being raised throughout the country as well as a rise in the quantity of eggs laid. This policy was applied in various ways to other industries. In was applied to the Chinese pig farmers who were supplied with pedigree pigs. There had also been a lot of research done on rice and the rice stock was also improved. What was happening was that everyone was becoming a little Capitalist and as such would want less and less to do with Communism.

Another radical program was introduced that had far reaching and beneficial effects. Much of the government land was occupied by Chinese squatters who used it to grow food crops. The Chinese terrorists obtained much of their food and money by coercion from these unfortunate victims. At that time Chinese were not allowed to own government land. This land was reserved for Malays only. In an unprecedented move the government granted these Chinese squatters ownership. In the political climate of the day this was a bold but very wise move. This action must certainly have inclined these new owners, formerly squatters, to take a more favourable view of the government and less of their compatriot Chinese terrorists. However there was still the problem of the terrorists threatening the farmers, demanding food and money from them, usually during a visit at night. To overcome this problem the government set up what were called New Villages into which the farmers and their families were moved. They lived in these new villages, sleeping there overnight and going out to work their land during the day. These new villages occupied a large area. Housing, better than the farmers had been using themselves, was built. Also all the facilities required in a village, such as schools, water supply, sanitation, medical facilities, etc. were all provided. Schooling and medical facilities had never previously been available to the squatters and their families. This provided a wonderful opportunity for their children to have a better future than their parents.

The whole area was fenced in, in order to keep the terrorists OUT. The Vietnamese government sent representatives to Malaya to study the system which was working so well and supposedly copied it when they returned. However, later on an inspection visit to Plantation Terre Rouge in Vietnam I noticed a marked difference in attitude and implementation. Where in Malaya the fences were to keep the terrorists out, in Vietnam they were used to keep the occupants IN. The occupants were being treated as potential enemies whereas in Malaya they were treated as potential friends needing protection. The result of this unfortunate distinction can be seen in the final outcome. Malaya eventually became a single united prosperous country, Malaysia, but Vietnam was split in two.

There was still the problem of the farmers being coerced into providing food to the terrorists. This was overcome in a way that brought unpredicted benefits to the farmers. The simple way to prevent food falling into the hands of the terrorists was to forbid it to be grown. The farmers were forbidden to grow foodstuffs and were only allowed to grow cash crops. The most popular cash crop was pepper. These cash crops truly did provide cash and it was not long before the farmers acquired considerable sums of money, far more than they had been accustomed to by growing their usual crops. So everyone was more than happy and more little capitalists were created to counteract the propaganda of the Chinese Communists who said that everyone would be better off under their rule where everyone would share their wealth.

As a final comment the New Villages were very well planned and many later developed into little townships that are still there to this day.

Weapons of Mass Destruction.

Some of you may recall that there was total agreement that weapons of mass destruction were held by Iraq. Later when the country was occupied and searches made for these weapons of mass destruction none were found. How was it that such (misleading) information could have been accepted as accurate? Here is one possibility.

I worked for an American company whose Head Office was in America. As General Manager I frequently paid visits to Head Office. At the time of this particular visit the "Domino Theory" was in favour. For those of you unfamiliar with the meaning of this term I will explain. America was going through a period when the fear of the spread of communism was dominant in their political thinking. This was also the time of McCarthyism. The communist influence was engulfing Korea and Vietnam. It was thought that if this" Domino effect" continued it was expected that Siam (now Thailand) and then Malaya, where there was already a communist insurgency, would eventually fall under the influence of communism.

On this particular visit I was told that the President of the company wished to see me to find out my views in regards to the Domino Effect and the general political situation in Southeast Asia. I was told that the President was a very busy man and that my interview would be limited 5 minutes. I was instructed to tell him that the Domino Effect was a real threat and unless some action was taken to prevent it both Siam (now Thailand) and Malaya (now Malaysia) would soon fall under the influence of communism. I was quite surprised that I should be told what to say to the President of the Company. I could now see why 5 minutes would be sufficient. There could be no stronger proof that he was being told what the most senior person thought he should be told and that if any of his junior staff did not comply with this view and spoke against it, it was more likely than not that they would lose their job. I was not his junior staff and furthermore was isolated from his influence. From past experience I knew the best thing was to say nothing about my intentions.

I was shown into the President's office and warmly greeted. After a few pleasantries he asked me for my views on the "Domino Effect". I started off by telling him what I have written under the heading above "WINNING HEARTS AND MINDS" and included many more interesting facts. He was fascinated and asked me many questions about the local situation. The interview lasted probably about 45 minutes way past their allotted 5 min. At the conclusion he thanked me and asked why he had not received such information before. I told him that if I had complied with his senior man's instructions he would have heard nothing new. On leaving his office the executive who had told me what to say during the interview could not believe that my interview had lasted 45 min or so – it was unprecedented. I do not know what action the President took after my departure but I am pretty sure he would have dealt with it in a strong and appropriate manner.

For some time after I kept thinking of the similarity between the situation of the President of my Company and that of the President of USA in regards to the supply of critical information. "Weapons of Mass Destruction –that were never found!" and what about Reports on situations in other parts of the world? Who can you trust?

Liberia..

During my time as General Manager I received a telegram asking me go to Monrovia the capital of Liberia to look into the possibility of acquiring two large land concessions one of which was being developed for rubber. I flew to London and then Paris as this was where I had to obtain a Liberian visa. Flying over the Sahara on my way to Liberia it was interesting to notice what almost appeared to be ancient riverbeds cut in the desert sands. On arrival in Monrovia I visited our agent and was flown by small plane, on about a two hour trip, to the Plantation to inspect the property. There was a small hospital with a doctor and small staff in attendance, which was very fortunate because I became extremely ill. My illness could not be diagnosed. Most of the time I was delirious. Even so it was considered in my best interests to try to treat me in the small estate hospital rather than be flown back by small aircraft to Monrovia. I recovered and after a few days of convalescence resumed light duties. We acquired the Plantations. On my return to Malaysia my dear wife, Nina, told me she had received information from our Head Office that it was possible that I would be returning in a Coffin.

Dumboy and Foo Foo.

On one occasion when, I was due to visit and inspect our Liberian Company, the Vice President suggested my wife accompany me on my trip both to Liberia and afterwards to our Head Office in America where I would present my report. This was a wonderful gesture and as America was halfway around the world from Malaya we took the opportunity to travel back via Los Angeles, Hawaii and Japan. On arrival at the Estate in Liberia we were both made very welcome. The senior staff there were all Americans with the exception of an assistant accountant who was Liberian. The field staff were all Dutch. The Americans imported all their food from America. As a welcoming gesture our host decided to put on a meal consisting of local dishes. This was the first time for both them and us to sample the local food. We found out that none of them had previously cooked or tried any local food and they thought this would be a wonderful opportunity for us and everyone else to try it out. As no one was able to cook local dishes they asked the wife of the Assistant Accountant, who was Liberian, to cook them. Two dishes were chosen. They were Dumboy and Foo Foo. One turned out to be very much like a Malayan curry and the other a sweet desert.

Nina and I had no trouble eating and enjoying these two delicious dishes. We were however, rather embarrassed to see our hosts hesitantly nibbling at small portions of, which to them was, unfamiliar and strange food especially as the Liberian Assistant Accountant and his wife who cooked the dishes were present. The evening went very well and we departed in very good spirits.

The next day it was planned I should visit the West Africa American Fruit Company to consider if it was worth acquiring. Nina was to accompany me on the one-hour plane trip. On arrival at the airstrip we were told by the pilot that as the rubber trees at the end of the runway had grown quite high he did not think that we could also take my wife as he did not have the previous length of runway for take-off. By coincidence and very fortunately there happened to be another small aircraft which had just landed. The pilot was a Dutch missionary who had removed all seats and was carrying a large number of Liberians back to the Estate. We chatted with him and found out that he was also looking after a leper colony and was visiting there that morning and would be back in the afternoon. When he found that Nina was not travelling with me he asked if she would like to visit the colony with him. He was probably expecting a refusal but she had already visited a similar leper colony at Pulau Jerjerak, off Penang Island, and so was quite pleased to accept the offer and gain more experience in the work, treatment and rehabilitation of people suffering from that disease.

We both took off about the same time. My trip was uneventful. However, because of the political situation in the country, the property had been badly neglected and it was not worth considering as an acquisition. On my return to the Estate I was amazed to find an ambulance waiting. As soon as the aircraft had landed and taxied to its resting place the medics rushed up to the plane. I disembarked and they immediately asked how I and my wife were. They did not know that she had gone off in another aircraft. I asked them why they were so concerned. They replied that all the expatriates who had been at the dinner the previous evening had suffered extreme diarrhoea and were all hospitalised and unable to go to work. They were sure it was because of the food that they had eaten the previous night. All day they had been extremely concerned that my wife and I were suffering from the same complaint with the added disadvantage of being cooped up in a small aircraft. I explained I had no after-effects at all and in fact was in quite good health. Their concern then centred on my wife. I stayed there with the ambulance fairly confident when she returned they would find her in the same good condition as I. This proved to be the case.

Immunisation ?

In my earlier days in Malaya I was living in remote areas and ate a lot of locally cooked dishes. When I first started doing so I suffered severe diarrhoea but in a short time I must have become "immunised" and never had this problem again no matter where I travelled and what I ate.

During my wife's time, residing in Malaysia, she more often than not would shop at the local market where she got to know many of the Malay and Chinese stall keepers. Many of our meals were local dishes. Often when we went out we would buy meals from roadside stalls. This was something not many of our compatriots did and in general not recommended. At first, like me, she suffered severe diarrhoea but with encouragement from me and my explaining to her how I had become immune to this problem she persevered. She also became immune and only on one other occasion, at a very special party, did she have that problem again. I think it was this past experience that saved us both from what could have been a catastrophe.

Retirement.

Soon after independence the government now Malaysia aimed to Malayanise all foreign companies as quickly as possible. This meant that companies had to replace foreign executives with Malaysians and eventually to have a majority

Malaysian ownership. Consequently I was forced to take early retirement in 1978,

My Second Career.

My New Consulting Job

The transmigration projects in Indonesia were having problems. These were very large schemes where jungle in remote isolated areas was cleared, and in this case, planted with rubber trees. An infrastructure was set up which included roads, bridges and areas of accommodation where all the facilities of a small village were provided – at first at a very basic level. There were several of these projects in Sumatra and one large one in East Kalimantan (Borneo). They were quasi government companies. Several of these plantations were running into difficulties and they required someone to solve the problem. My name had been put forward as a potential consultant to help solve these problems. A meeting was arranged in Kuala Lumpur for me to meet the Indonesian representatives. I was surprised at the magnitude of the projects and also of the magnitude of the problems. The size of the planting done in a year on these projects were in some cases as large as a whole estate in Malaysia. The main problem was the low rate of success in transplanting rubber stumps from the nursery to the field. The percentage was unbelievably low, so low in fact that I could only offer to visit the projects to see if I was capable of solving the problem. This suggestion was agreed to and I spent the next two to three weeks visiting several projects in Indonesia. By the end of my visit I had diagnosed the problem and was confident that it could be quickly solved. I accepted their offer to work as their Consultant and spent the next ten years travelling back and forth from Indonesia first to Penang and later to Australia, working on these projects.

The Employees.

The employees housed on these projects were a real mixture. None had any agricultural or plantation experience. They were made up of ex-military and ex-police who had finished their five or ten years of service and did not wish to continue in that line of duty but had no other source of employment. There were also large numbers of unemployed, mainly from overpopulated Java, who were willing to move, with their families, to these remote areas and start a new life and take up a new and unfamiliar occupation.

The Transmigration Projects.

On each project there was an area with housing and each house might have as much as three acres attached. The house was very primitive by any standards yet the new occupants were astonished and delighted to become the owners. The extra land provided with the house was meant for growing food crops, raising poultry and in most cases some cash crops as well so that the occupants could become self-sufficient. For the first year assistance was given in the way of food, mainly rice.

Nurseries were set up into which rubber seeds were planted. When they were big enough they were grafted with high yielding buds and left to grow for about another year. These "stumps" were then pulled out, delivered to the transmigrants to be replanted into what was to become a large communal Plantation. When the rubber trees were large enough to be tapped the Plantation was divided into individual plots of about three acres in size and each transmigrant became the owner of the land and trees in that unit. This was all paid for by the government. However, the idea was that once rubber was being harvested and sold a percentage of the income from the sales would return to the government as repayment for what they had outlaid to establish the projects. This could then be used towards new projects. This was an excellent scheme and provided much employment to those most in need. The resulting smoke created by the burning of such large areas of felled jungle was often noticed as far away as,what was now known as Malaysia.

Incidentally, using chain saws, some of these felled trees were cut into planks to provide building material for the houses. These houses were in most cases later whitewashed.

Identifying the Problem.

There were many problems to be resolved. But the main one which was causing the large lack of success in transplanting the rubber stumps into the field was quickly resolved.

None of the occupants were farmers and none had any agriculture experience. The procedure was that each day a delivery of fifty stumps, pulled from the nursery and tied in bundles, would be made to each family. This was rather a small amount to plant and could be done very quickly. It was expected that each delivery would be immediately planted and on this assumption no protection to the planting material was provided.

What was happening was that, because the number of stumps delivered per family was so small, they were being kept for several days until there was a sufficient quantity to provide a reasonable day's work for the family. Consequently, with the possible exception of the last day's delivery the stumps had dried out and had no chance of survival.

The Solution.

I called my managers together and explained my diagnosis. We visited one of the units where I wished to demonstrate to all the occupants what they were doing wrong. I took with me a few rubber seedlings which I placed on a table in front of me. With such a large group of unskilled, and for the most part uneducated, workers a special approach was needed. Being technical would not produce any results. I started off by telling them that the seedlings were baby rubber trees just like their children. I knew they all looked after their children in the hope that when they were grown up they would be looked after by them in their old age. It was the same with rubber seedlings. If they looked after them when they were babies then when they grew up they would provide them with an income in their old age.

I asked them if they would leave their baby in the back room or out in the sun for several days without water or shade. The reply was a unanimous "NO". I told them but this what they were doing with their planting material which were baby rubber trees. Once their roots dried out the plants were dead transplanting them would not bring them back to life. I think the message was very clear.

To emphasise what I had said I then showed them the seedlings I had brought with me which, having been in the full sun for almost an hour and a half with their roots exposed were now wilting.

From then on when the stumps were pulled from the nursery they were protected with damp sacking and delivered in the same way. They were transplanted on the day of arrival. The success rate jumped to almost 100%.

The Staff

I found all the staff on the transmigration projects extremely helpful in understanding our objectives and was pleased that they did such a wonderful job in such a short time. It was a pleasure to work with them and I am very grateful to have been part of the transmigration projects in Indonesia.

Final Retirement.

Finally the time came to really retire. For the last ten years, whilst working in Indonesia, I had been spending about three months on the Plantations with a two week break travelling back and forth, first to our home in Penang and later, when the family moved to Australia to Perth. I had been doing a lot of travelling not only back and forth but also in Indonesia and the time came for me to finally decide to have a full social life in retirement. So in 1988 I finally said farewell to my friends in Indonesia and returned home to Perth to live a normal life.

Our Farm.

It didn't quite turn out that way. Nina and I bought a farm near Beverly and from 1989 to 2002 ran 600 to 800 sheep, fattening them and turning them over two to three times a year. We did the fencing, drenching, spraying and other manual work.

Margaret and Phil in Shearing Shed

We also share farmed with our neighbour. We would spend a few days a week on the farm.

There was also a dilapidated farm house on the property and we spent a year, together with the family, renovating it. We did the roof, fixed all the leaks, damp proofed the walls repainted everything and sanded and polished the beautiful Jarrah floors. We ended up with a beautiful house and it was there in March 2002 that my dear wife suddenly and unexpectedly suffered a severe stroke. An ambulance took us to Perth where she passed away later in the afternoon with all her family present, just over two weeks after celebrating our fiftieth wedding Anniversary. It happened to be a public holiday and I was able, before leaving the farm, to notify all the children that we were on our way Royal Perth Hospital .

A year later I sold the farm.

PART 3

THE WAR PERIOD

The Royal Airforce.

I was born in Portsmouth England in 1922. On completing my schooling I won a Bursary Scholarship to study for a Bachelor of Science at Bristol University. As the war had started I gave up my studies and volunteered to join the Royal Air Force as a Pilot. I was eventually called for an interview and having passed this I underwent a medical examination which I passed. In addition to the usual tests I was checked for colour blindness and my ability to see in the dark. I also had a dental check and for the first time in my life had fillings put in three of my teeth. I was sent home to await advice on my first posting. At about the age of 15 my parents thought I should wear glasses and took me to an optometrist who prescribed them for me. Against all my upbringing I refused to wear them. Had I done so I would never have been able to have applied to become a Pilot in the R.A.F. and my whole future and even my personality would have been completely different to what it is now.

My first posting was to St John's Wood in London. Here we were supplied with uniforms and prepared for posting to our first unit to begin our flying training. We were all young and fit but during our short stay at Saint John's Wood all of us complained of lack of libido. Rumour had it that the tea served to us was laced with bromide, which we understood, acted as an anti-aphrodisiac. I can well believe this because the tea had an unusual and unpleasant taste. The authorities were obviously aiming to reduce the chances of any inappropriate behaviour taking place amongst such a large group of young healthy and virile men living in such cramped quarters. About two weeks later I, together with a few others, was posted to Saint Andrews in Scotland where we received basic training in Meteorology, Navigation, Engines and other required subjects.

The short stay there was very agreeable. We all became very good friends and often in the evenings a small group of us would do a "Pub Crawl". The usual drink was a Scotch and Chaser, the chaser being a beer. This was a potent mixture so our Pub Crawls did not last too long

The Committee of the prestigious Saint Andrews Golf Club, as a patriotic gesture, opened the course to us servicemen free of charge. The club house was a large and most impressive building. It would have served well as the manor for a wealthy Lord. We must have been amongst the only people in the world who, without a golf handicap and never having held a golf club in their lives, were allowed to play on these prestigious and renowned links.

I also recall swimming in the sea in mid-December. It was a cold but sunny day and there were ice crystals forming along the shore. I was the only one foolish enough to do so.

Our training continued and those who successfully completed this basic course were sent South to learn to fly and carry out their first solo flight. The aircraft used for training was the Tiger Moth, a very forgiving 'plane. Even today I vividly recall my first solo. As soon as I realised I was up off the ground, flying through the air, all on my own, I started yelling out in uncontrolled excitement. A little later the thought of having to land the 'plane suddenly dawned on me. This somewhat dampened my initial excitement. However, I carried out a perfect landing. The pure joy and pleasure of that moment was something never to be forgotten. Later we also carried out simulated parachute jumps from a tower.

Another very interesting aspect of our training, which revealed that we had amazing powers of memory, was that we had to memorise all the aircraft and battleships of the allied forces and our enemies. This was obviously necessary to avoid the possibility of us attacking our own aircraft and warships. To do this we used packs of "Flip Cards". A sketch of the aircraft or warship that we had to memorise was on one side and the name of the aircraft or vessel and the country to which it belonged was on the other. It is amazing how in a very short time we became adept at memorising so many aircraft and warships.

Those of us who completed the course satisfactorily were selected for further training. Those who failed returned to ordinary duties. This weeding-out process continued throughout our training and we were frequently saying farewell to many good friends.

Posting Overseas.

Flying training was not safe in the UK so advanced flying training was conducted overseas under what was known as the Empire Training Scheme. Posting could be to Canada, Australia, South Africa and a few other safe havens. My posting was an exception. I, with a few others, was sent to America, via Canada. America at that time was not at war but had offered to help the UK train it's pilots together with their own American Army Air Force personnel. I did my advanced flying training at an American Air Base outside Ponca City in Oklahoma. The second day after our arrival a large number of local inhabitants arrived on the base. We soon learned the reason. They were to become our Foster parents. I was taken under the wing of the Knight family, who had a young son suffering from polio. They were a wonderful friendly family and I was frequently invited to participate with them in a family meal and outings. I was also invited to drop in any time I wanted. After I left I kept in touch with these wonderful and generous people for many years. Just before the end of the war I lost touch with them. Perhaps they had moved, perhaps they had died. I do not know the reason.

My memories of my stay in Ponca City have faded but I do remember two special ones. The first was that "Blacks", as they were then called, and Red Indians, off the neighbouring reservation, were not allowed in bars, hotels or restaurants. If they were allowed on certain busses they had to sit in the back. In spite of this discrimination, some of the Red Indians could be seen driving around town in Cadillac's, presumably bought with money received as royalties from the oil found on their reservations.

The other memory was being shown over a Research Centre belonging to one of the large Oil Companies. Here, among other things, we were shown a clear liquid. It did not stick to the glass test tube. It was predicted that, if development went as expected, it would be a super cleaner and could replace soap. Although we did not know it at the time, this was to become the now well-known "detergent". None of us of course realised the potential of this material. It was not till many years later when I came across a door to door salesman trying to promote the sale of a new unknown washing liquid, detergent, that past memories of my visit in Ponca City surfaced.

Flying Training.

One of the first things demonstrated to us, on our arrival at our base in Ponca City, was how to use a parachute. We had already been trained in the use of parachutes in the UK, where we had practiced simulated drops from towers. However, I presume for the sake of thoroughness, this item was again included in our course. We started with the instructor standing on a table surrounded by us, his pupils. He showed us how to put the harness on and then how to use the rip cord to open the parachute in the event of an emergency. When he pulled the ripcord nothing happened. He called for a second parachute. He pulled the ripcord. Again nothing happened. We were not impressed; our instructor was most embarrassed. The class was dismissed and instructions given for all parachutes on the base to be repacked. So it was just as well that a demonstration had been given otherwise the poor state of the parachutes might never have been discovered.

At our American base we had, once more, to go through the process of carrying out a Solo flight, this time on a new more powerful aircraft, the Stearman. The starting method was, to us, unique. You stood on the tarmac next to the 'plane. You inserted a handle into a hole in the side of the aircraft. This was attached to a heavy flywheel mechanism. You started to turn the handle. Due to inertia this required quite an effort and slowly but surely the mighty flywheel would gather speed and the pitch of the whirring flywheel would slowly rise. At the appropriate time the handle was removed, you hopped into the pilot's seat, clicked a switch which then linked the flywheel to the engine which then rotated the propeller and started the engine.

Here again many of our friends dropped out and were sent back to England. Having accomplished our second "solo" flight and some more basic training we graduated to a more powerful aircraft, the Harvard. This aircraft was in many respects similar to the single engine fighter aircraft, the Mustang. Training continued and included flying on instruments, formation flying, low flying and advanced navigation.

Later in the course we carried out a long triangular cross-country flight. My best friend, one of the Americans, was co-pilot. We were near our destination when we were enveloped in thick cloud. The area around the city was very mountainous. We consulted one another as to when it might be safe to descend. Eventually we decided to drop down below cloud level. Coming out of the clouds we saw green stretches of farmland well below us and our destination in the far distance. We were very pleased with our navigational skills. Then my friend looked back and was horrified to see a sheer wall of rock rising up into the clouds. If we had started our descent a few minutes earlier we would have hit the ground without ever knowing what had happened.

This same friend lost his life in a crash during training and was given a Military Funeral. I do not know how this happened but to this day I have a guilty feeling that I might have been responsible. I had successfully done an inverted spin. I told him about what I had done. The next day he crashed and was killed. At the time I did not connect the two but many years later it dawned on me he might have tried the inverted spin and failed to come out of it.

I thoroughly enjoyed flying. I spent a lot of time doing aerobatics. On one occasion while I was leader flying in low level flying formation I unlocked my Joy Stick, took it out and waved it to my flight companions on my left and right.

During my final flying test, with my instructor, I asked him, while flying under the hood and on instruments, if I could do a barrel roll. He agreed and I did a very good roll. I had of course been practicing this on nearly all my training flights.

On the last day of our training we were all sent up into the air with gun cameras where we spent time engaged in mock dog fights.

At the end of the course I passed out with the rank of Pilot Officer. I also received a certificate nominating me as top pilot. This certificate is still amongst my belongings.

Hitchhiking to Mexico.

Before being posted back to England, we were given two weeks leave. A friend, John, and I decided we would hitchhike to Mexico and back. The first people who picked us up thought we were US Marines, perhaps because our uniform was of similar colour. They were a middle aged to elderly couple well dressed and very friendly. At this time America was not at war. When they found out that we were Royal Air Force trainee pilots their welcome and hospitality knew no bounds. They took us to a restaurant and ordered an excellent meal. It was here I had my first experience of Tabasco sauce, a very spicy condiment. After the meal they asked us if we would like to stay with them overnight before proceeding on our way. The hospitality and welcome we received from these people, who gave us our first lift, was unbelievable. It was repeated on every occasion during the whole of our two weeks leave. We were invited to stay in their houses, we were taken out to meals, in fact everywhere we went we were treated like long lost relatives. There can be no doubt of the warmth of feeling of the Americans for their English cousins fighting the war in Europe.

We had not appreciated the huge distances involved when travelling in America. As a consequence we soon realised that, with the time taken meeting so many new friends, plus the consequent stopovers we were making on the way, it would take much more time than we had at our disposal to reach Mexico. To achieve our objective of getting to Mexico and back, in the two weeks available, we needed a faster means of transport. We decided to call in at a U.S. Army Air Base and see if they would be willing to give us a lift in an aircraft going that way. Today, to even contemplate such an idea would be inconceivable. However at that time it seemed to us a normal thing to do. When we arrived at the base and had explained who we were and why we had called in, we were greeted with open arms. No questions were asked, no proof of identity was required, no security checks, just our word and that we were in uniform was enough. How times have changed! That afternoon there was a plane going to a base outside of Laredo on the Mexican border. The pilot told us we were welcome to join them and so we had our first flight in a Flying Fortress.

The next day we crossed the crowded old bridge over the Rio Grande into Nueva Laredo Mexico. No checks, no passports required. The first thing we did was very Mexican. We sat down at a typical small Mexican roadside café and ordered Tequila, the national drink of Mexico. It was served up with, what we later learned was, the customary accompanying lemon and salt.

We return to Europe.

At the end of our leave we returned to Ponca City and prepared ourselves for our return to England. We said farewell to our "Foster parents" and to our many wonderful friends. When we arrived at the station to board our train it appeared as if the whole town had turned out to bid us farewell. It was like a fair ground with people milling around everywhere. It was a very emotional scene with hugs being exchanged and the occasional tear being shed. As the train pulled out there were waving farewells and resounding cheers which gradually faded away as we disappeared into the distance.

I cannot remember the name of the ship that took us back to England. I believe it might have been the Otranto. It had previously been a cruise ship and now had been converted into a troop carrier. Every nook and cranny was used to accommodate a human body. The ship was completely overloaded. Almost everywhere on the lower decks there were provisions for hammocks. These took up very little space and so more bodies could be packed in. Most of us, including myself, were to experience for the first time the "delight" of sleeping in a hammock. We put them up at night and took them down during the day.

We set sail to Europe zigzagging all the way to make us a more difficult target for lurking U-Boats. On the second day we encountered a severe storm. I can vouch that this was a beauty. Almost everyone was seasick. I fortunately was one of the very few not affected. This was not much consolation as all the basins, toilets and urinals were blocked and the smell throughout the lower decks was intolerable. During the voyage we were posted, throughout the ship, on sentry duty, armed with a rifle. Shifts were 4 hour on 8 hours off 24 hours a day. I recall, during the storm, being posted well forward. The bow, ploughing through the monstrous waves caused it to heave upward and then down. When the bow went down I would almost leave the deck on which I was standing and the rifle became as light as a feather. Under the circumstances carrying out guard duty seemed a ridiculous, unnecessary and a futile exercise but I expect it was done with the intention of maintaining discipline and keeping us occupied.

It was when we berthed and found how slow, difficult and long it took for such a large number of troops to disembark that I realised if we had been torpedoed very few of us would have had any chance whatsoever of getting out of what would have become a watery tomb.

Map Reading in Europe.

One of the first things we had to do on our arrival in England was to familiarize ourselves with flying over the English countryside. In the area in America where we had trained, the roads were far apart in grids running north and south, and east and west. The cities were located fairly far apart and little or no skill was required in map reading. You just followed the road or the train line to get to your destination. The situation was totally different in England and Europe. Therefore on arrival in England we were posted to our respective air bases to do a short course in map reading by flying over the English countryside, which was also similar to that in Europe.

When we were considered proficient at map reading, we were sent to a base in southeast England to await posting to a squadron. On my way I had inadvertently gone to a place with a similar name to that of my official destination and so arrived late at my proper destination. As a consequence I was grouped with a unit made up of men from various colonial forces. These consisted mainly of Australian, New Zealand, South African and others. We were a small but mixed bunch and got on exceedingly well.

Phil in Uniform.

One of the special exercises allotted the unit, probably to pass time, was a simulated operation to seek out German air crew that might have parachuted out of shot-down aircraft. As we were a small unit, six of us, including myself, were selected to be the enemy. We were told it was forbidden to take any money with us and that before we departed we would be searched. We would be dressed in uniforms similar to that worn by the German Luftwaffe. We would be driven out in a bus with curtained windows so that we would not know where we were going and be "dropped" somewhere in the countryside. The whole unit would then be sent out to comb the area and capture us. It was our objective to get back to base without being caught. It all sounded great fun. The operation would start on the following day.

The morrow arrived. We turned out dressed in our distinctive new uniforms. We were thoroughly searched for money. Our shoes were removed, No money was found. We were loaded into the bus and driven to where we did not know. On arrival we were "dropped" in the countryside. The bus left with the driver shouting out "Good luck chaps".

The whole unit would start a big sweep of the countryside looking for us, starting at approximately the same time we were dropped off. Time was on our side. We took off our shoes then our socks and removed a few good sized denomination Bank of England notes that were hidden in them. No one had thought of asking us to remove our socks! We discussed whether or not we should remove our distinctive jackets. As we only had vests underneath and it was winter, we decided that would make us too conspicuous as well as uncomfortable. We started out walking along the road until we came to our first manhole. Sign posts had been removed. There written indelibly on the metal cover, for all to see, was the district and the name of the nearby town. Immediately we knew where we were and also that the nearest village would not be too far away. After a short walk we arrived at the village. We brazenly decided to drop into the local pub for a drink. Our entrance created not even the trace of a stir. We approached the bar and ordered a pint of mild and bitter each. "Coming up Sir" said the barman. We sat there comfortably ensconced on our bar stools, in warm surroundings, and marvelled at our good fortune in having been the chosen as the foxes in this game of the Fox and Hounds. About an hour or so must have passed when we noticed though the window, troops fanned out moving through the village obviously searching for us. As Lady Luck favours the bold no one thought of looking in the pub. After all who in their right mind, under such circumstances, would enter such a public place? The troops soon passed out of sight. A quarter of an hour later we thought it time to move on. We left with a friendly farewell to the barman. We proceeded fairly swiftly on our walk back to base, comforted by the fact that we would meet with no opposition, as our enemy was many miles away and moving in a direction that rapidly increased the distance between us. We arrived back at base to be greeted with a certain amount of surprise as well as congratulations. They were a bit puzzled by how all of us had managed to return back to base together and not be apprehended. The authorities never debriefed us as they obviously thought we had managed to get back by hiding in bushes and avoiding all public places. Later in front of the whole unit we were commended while the search groups were told they had failed dismally by not even capturing one of us.

For many years I wondered how was it possible that, dressed in a uniform similar to the Luftwaffe, six of us could enter a pub and just sit there drinking beer and not be challenged or apprehended. I put it down to two possible reasons. The first is that we all spoke good English, some with an Aussie or New Zealand accent and we acted in a normal carefree manner. The second is the occupants of the British Isles were accustomed to seeing a variety of uniforms. These included Free French, Free Polish and other foreign troops who had escaped from the Nazi's and who could be seen moving around the country often in strange and unfamiliar uniforms. Of course, at the time, none of us had the slightest idea what would happen when we walked into that pub many years ago.

I also now recall, how in America, during our training we had gone on leave dressed in unfamiliar uniform and had been accepted for what we said we were by all and sundry without exception, even to the point of being given a lift by the US Army Air Force in one of their Flying Fortresses. Times have indeed changed.

A Change of Occupation.

Later in the war, at Arnhem, (A bridge too far) the Glider Regiment was much depleted. To make up the losses of these trained men as quickly as possible the Army and Air force came up with a novel solution. Some of us were given the opportunity to volunteer as Glider Pilots. I was one of those who volunteered. With our flying skills we (Officer Pilot and Sergeant Co-pilot) only required one dual then one solo day flight and one night flight each to master the art of landing safely on the right spot without an engine. Our first flights were in Hengist or Horsa gliders. They were very small and only carried a few men. After that we graduated to Hamilcars. In comparison these appeared massive and could carry a large number of troops and equipment. We had large concrete blocks placed in them to simulate a load. They had flaps the size of barn doors and could come down almost vertical and stop in an extremely short distance, which of course was essential for safety in combat zones.

One of the jobs of the co-pilot was to release the glider at the exact time chosen by the pilot of the glider so he would be able to land in the right spot. The tow 'plane was NEVER to release the glider. The command was "Get ready for release", this was followed by the command to drop the tow rope which was "OK". One of our group, when being instructed in this procedure, was told "when you get the command "OK" pull the release lever"....OK? He mistook the question as a command and released the glider. They landed in a farmer's field with a ton of concrete aboard. The instructor was not amused.

On completion of this short training course we were immediately shipped off to India to take part in the Burma Campaign. We were flown from UK to Karachi via El Aden, in North Africa and then Basrah. In those days 'planes could not make the long non-stop flights they are capable of doing nowadays. From Karachi we were flown to our base at nearby Fatehjang. There was practically nothing at Fatehjang closely resembling a base. It was a primitive stop-over. Whilst there we nearly all experienced the delights of, what we fondly called, "The Himalayan Trots"; in more mundane terms diarrhea. The "trots" being what we performed when trotting back and forth to the make-shift fly infested latrines.

At Fatehjang we were introduced to a new glider known as the WACO. This was to become the standard glider used in all the major operations of the war. We piloted these gliders in one hop across the whole of northern India to a base near Calcutta. Our gliders were towed in pairs by DC3s also known as Dakotas. My companion pilot was always Vic. We became very good and close friends. One glider would fly low on the right the other high on the left. I usually took the low right.

From our base near Calcutta we were sent by train back across the width of India to Belgaum to undergo a crash Red Beret course and learn some basic Hindustani. The train trip took several days and the conditions were hot, cramped and uncomfortable. At intervals, when the train stopped, we would get down and run up to the engine driver with a bucket. Most of the drivers were Anglo Indians and spoke good English. "Can we have some hot water for *char* (tea)" we would ask. "Sure" they would reply. We would put the bucket on the ground near the steam outlet pipe. The driver would pull a lever and our bucket would be filled with boiling water in an instant. We would take it back to our carriage and put in tea leaves, wrapped in a cloth, to make a large quantity of refreshing tea.

On one occasion, while filling a bucket, I asked the driver if I could drive the train. He was very obliging. He told me that once we had left the station he would stop the train. "Come up as quickly as possible," he said, and you can drive the train until we get close to the next station where I will stop so you can go back to your carriage. A short while after leaving the station he stopped the train. I ran up to the engine and climbed into the drivers' cabin. Driving was a piece of cake. He showed me the lever to pull and how far to pull it. I was ready for my solo "flight". I pulled the lever and felt the mighty weight of the train and all the carriages move forward under my control. I "drove" the train for many miles. Just before we arrived at the next station my good friend told me to slow down. I did so and we came to a stop. I disembarked ran back to board my carriage and waved for him to continue. I could fly a plane and glider and had now driven a train and still had never driven a car!

After our crash Red Beret training course with the army was finished we travelled back across the width of India to join up with our army Glider Regiment counterparts. Our unit was known as the CCTF or Combat Cargo Task Force, whose job it was to ferry in troops and equipment to combat areas and take part in the conflict or if feasible treck back to base in order to bring in more gliders with troops and/or equipment. Towards the end of the war I believe a scheme was devised to try and recover and bring back the gliders landed during an operation. A continuous loop of nylon towing cable was attached to the glider and then to the top of two poles located in front of and to the left and right of the glider. The towplane was to come over dragging a nylon towing line behind it to which a hook was attached in an attempt to pick up the line attached to the two poles. I only heard of this proposal and do not know for certain if such a manoeuvre was ever attempted.

During all our years together we kept our RAF uniforms and the army kept theirs. On parade we looked an unusual mob.

At an Air Force base just outside of Calcutta we saw our old friend the Hamilcar. We never flew them. To the best of my knowledge this may have been because in the humidity and heat experienced in the tropics the glue used in their construction failed. At that time epoxy resins had not been developed. So, instead of using Hamilcars, we used the American WACO which was a steel framed glider covered with canvas. The parts for these were shipped out in crates and assembled on arrival. As well as troops they could carry a jeep or other small vehicle. A real Heath Robinson system was used to unload the vehicle, usually a jeep, from the glider when it landed. A wire cable ran from the rear of the jeep up to the roof along it then ran through a pulley back down to where it was attached to the to the cockpit. The whole cockpit was hinged along the top. As soon as the glider stopped, the co-pilot pulled a lever which unlocked the lower part of the cockpit. The driver of the jeep then drove his vehicle forward. In doing so the cockpit, with the two pilots strapped in their seats, was lifted up and outward on the upper hinges and locked there, allowing the jeep to drive out the front of the glider, followed by the troops. The pilots were left to their own devices to free themselves and get back down on the ground.

On one occasion we were sent to an American Air Base at Dum Dum, outside Calcutta, to test newly assembled WACO's. Several had been assembled with crossed controls so the Base Commander decided that the assemblers should, periodically, fly on a test flight as passengers to make them more aware of their responsibilities. I took one load of American servicemen up on such a flight. They were all equipped with parachutes which, in the event of an accident, would have been impossible to use and only added unnecessary weight. We, the pilot and co-pilot, were never supplied with parachutes. I do not know to this day what possessed me but, after we had pulled the release lever separating us from our tow plane, I decided to loop the fully loaded glider. I put the nose down and, when I considered we had gathered enough speed, gradually pulled the nose up and performed a perfect full loop of the fully manned glider. I do not know if the glider was designed for such treatment but I do know that if I had not performed a perfectly smooth loop none of us would have survived. The Glider Regiment Training Course would not have included aerobatics, as our RAF training had, so I do not know if anyone else ever attempted to perform this feat. Sometime after the war I tried to contact the manufactures of this amazing aircraft to tell them of this maneuver. Later I even used the internet, to try to make contact to ask about this but I could not do so. I believe the factory had closed.

We were always towed, in pairs, by a
DC3 also known as a Dakota.

Below is a Photo of the type of Glider used when I was with The Combat Cargo Task Force.
(We had different markings).

A Quote from

General William C. Westmoreland, U.S.
Army, Retired"

The intrepid pilots who flew the gliders were as unique as their motorless flying machines. Never before in history had any nation produced aviators whose duty it was deliberately to crash land, and then go on to fight as combat infantrymen. They were no ordinary fighters. Their battlefields were behind enemy lines." "Every landing was a genuine do-or-die situation for the glider pilots. It was their awesome responsibility to repeatedly risk their lives by landing heavily laden aircraft containing combat soldiers and equipment in unfamiliar fields deep within enemy-held territory, often in total darkness. They were the only aviators during World War II who had no motors, no parachutes, and no second chances.

A PHOTO TAKEN FROM MY GLIDER.

I served the rest of the war in the Burma Campaign with the CCTF (Combat Cargo Task Force).

Shot down Japanese Zero fighter.

The most interesting group of troops I carried were East African infantry who had come out by ship and had never been in an aircraft before, let alone a glider. During this period I also spent a short time with the friendly Naga Hill Tribesmen. The only animal that concerned them was the elephant. This was because if elephants were in the near vicinity and got wind of humans they could panic. Then there was no way of knowing where they would run and no one wanted to be trampled by a wild elephant. I recall surprising my co-pilot with a demonstration of my tracking skills. The incident occurred whilst trekking back to base along an elephant track in tall elephant grass. We were both quite exhausted and sopping wet with sweat. He was lagging behind when I came across a large round dollop of elephant dung right in the middle of the path. "The elephant must have only just passed here" I said. "How the hell do you know" he asked? "Simple" I said. "It is still steaming".

A few months before the Atom Bomb was dropped we were told that we would be carrying out a special large scale operation into Burma over the Arakan mountains. In anticipation of this we were sent on a mountaineering course into Ladahk which borders North West Tibet. We set out from our base camp by horse. Because we were living at high altitudes, at times of over 12,000 ft, we were allowed, against all RAF regulations, to grow a beard. This was to mitigate the effects of ultra violet light on our skin, which was extra strong at these high altitudes. I grew a beard and looked like Desperate Dan.

Vic and Phil   At about 15,000 ft HIMALAYAS

During this period, of about three weeks, we had no communication with the outside world. It was with amazement, great joy and relief to find, that when we got back to civilization, the war had ended. The atom bomb had brought the war in the Far East to a sudden and unexpected conclusion.

After the war finished I was offered a class B (immediate) release from the services in order to continue my University studies. I could not imagine myself settling into such a dull routine again and declined the offer. So instead of an immediate release it would be another six months before I was demobilised.

After the war was over, and I had declined my early release, there was no further need for our flying skills. Consequently we were offered a variety of miscellaneous jobs. In my case I was posted to Cocos Keeling Island to take charge of the Staging Post there. Cocos Island consists of a series of small islands only a few feet above sea level and about a few hundred yards wide and all of varying lengths, surrounding what might have been an extinct volcano. Here I spent about 5 months. The Staging Post was on West Island.

Aircraft flying from Ceylon, now Sri Lanka stopped there on their way to Perth, Australia.

There was also a small island, a triangular piece of sand, a few hundred meters wide, called Direction Island, on which there was the Cable and Wireless station.

COCOS KEELING ISLAND
Taken on arrival

Occasionally, on invitation from the Cable and wireless staff, a friend and I would sail over to Direction Island for a curry. We would arrange for one of the local inhabitants of "Home Island" to take us there in their dugongs, as the local sailing boats were known. One of our Direction Island friends name was Funnel pronounced Fernel. We often called him Funnel, like on a ship, much to his annoyance and our amusement. Early shades of Mrs. Bucket (Bouquet)!

A few of us used to go out fishing with the local inhabitants who all resided on Home Island. Their open sailing boats were quite unique. They carried up to 4 people. Sand bags were used as ballast which they moved around to keep the boat on an even keel when sailing in strong winds. The most common fish we caught, trolling our lines, were flying fish which were very tasty. Another pastime was, at night, to walk out between the reef and shore looking for crayfish. These were big and plentiful. There were also numerous small sharks which we never bothered and they never bothered us. Both of us obviously lacked experience. Before leaving shore we would light a fire under a 200 gallon oil drum full of water to cook our anticipated catch. We always caught enough to last us a week or so. It was easy. We found them on the sea bed asleep. We got a grip around their body, using our gloved hands, and popped them into our kit bag.

It is a strange commentary on human nature that we were always expected to share our hard earned catch. Our reply was, "If you want to eat crayfish you are welcome to join us any night we go out catching them". No one, yes NO ONE, ever took us up on our offer, Yet they continued to consider us selfish for not sharing.

Supplies for the few hundred troops stationed on Cocos Island were, I believe, only delivered about once each 6 months. This had serious consequences on our bread supply. The flour store could not be cleaned out between deliveries and consequently became a breeding ground for weevils. Our bread always looked as if it had an oversupply of caraway seed in it – which of course were weevils. Daily baking of bread still continued and we duly ate it. High protein bread we called it. There were however compensations. Gin was less than five shillings and a bottle and wine and beer correspondingly cheap.

From Cocos I was posted to Hong Kong. We were ferried to a boat anchored off Cocos Island and then sailed to Singapore via the Sunda Straits. On the way we passed the infamous Krakatau. In the 1800's, half the Island was blown away by a monstrous volcanic eruption. The shock waves were heard thousands of miles away. The large quantity of ash blown into the stratosphere travelled all over the globe creating beautiful and amazing sunsets for many months to come. From Singapore three other RAF officers and boarded a plane to Hong Kong. The Air Force plane we travelled in only went as far as Saigon, now called Ho Chi Min city. We stayed there for three nights before being transported by another RAF plane to Hong Kong.

SAIGON.

During our stay in Saigon we stayed at the RAF mess. After settling into our rooms we met in the bar for refreshments. We asked for beer. We were surprised to be offered either Shlitz or Pabst beer in cans, both well known American brands. We were also told that if there was any wax in the beer, bring it back and exchange it for another for free. The price was about a quarter the cost of a normal beer bought in an Officers Mess. We asked the barman how this had come about. He told us the story. There had been a fire in the American PX- their equivalent of the NAAFI. Their stock of beer, which consisted of cans of American beer packed in cardboard packs had been in the fire. They had opened a few cans and found that the inside wax coating had melted. They considered the beer undrinkable. They had put the whole lot up for auction. There was little opposition from the locals at that time and RAF had bought the whole lot for a song. The officer in charge of the RAF mess had either realized, from experience, that the outside cases acted as an insulator for the large number of cases in the middle; or he had taken a chance all would be well. I am inclined the former view. He was right in his assumption. In fact some of the inner cans in the outside packs were free of wax. We had a great time for very little expense.

On our second day we discovered that there was a bar and Dance Hall at Cholon, a suburb of Saigon. That evening we hired a taxi to take us there. We travelled through quite a bit of countryside before reaching our destination. Interestingly enough on a subsequent visit, many years later, Saigon had grown and engulfed Cholon. We arrived to find the place full of what appeared to be French Foreign Legionnaires and Taxi Dancers. Taxi Dancers are local girls who, for a fee, danced with customers. Customers bought tickets and gave one ticket per dance to the girl of his choice.

The hall was large and undecorated. The furniture was basic consisting of simple wooden chairs and tables. The most notable feature was a huge bar with every conceivable drink stacked on shelves behind it. Behind this array of drinks was a huge mirror spreading the length of the bar. It gave the appearance of doubling the already vast amount of drink available. The other notable feature was a small band of local musicians who seemed to be playing nonstop for the benefit of patrons as well as Taxi Dancers.

By their raucous behavior, it was obvious that some quite serious drinking had been going on for some time before our arrival. The Legionnaires were boisterous and many were very drunk. We had just sat down at a table for four and started on our drinks when a scuffle broke out at the far end of the hall. The next thing I remember was one of the soldiers, dressed in French Foreign Legion uniform, shouting "Achtung" and throwing a bottle at the shelves of drinks behind the bar. There was the sound of breaking glass as bottles broke, spilling their contents onto the floor and the large mirror behind the bar appeared to disintegrate in slow motion. I recall most vividly hearing the shrill screams of women. I turned round to see the diminutive Vietnamese women dressed in their beautiful and attractive silk dresses rushing out through the exit doors with the local band hot on their heels. In the blink of an eye the whole place was cleared of the local Taxi Dancers and musicians leaving behind only our European compatriots, the French Foreign Legionnaires.

The scuffle developed into a full fight and the localized fight spread rapidly throughout the dance hall. Tables were knocked over and chairs thrown in all directions, some coming close. We decided, most definitely, that we should leave immediately but would do so in a dignified manner. The four of us, for a short while, sat calmly in the midst of this bedlam. We ignored what was going on around us, drank our drinks speedily but without undue haste and left as soon as possible. We had maintained our dignity and also that of the armed force to which we belonged. We never found out how the fighting ended. We did learn however why it started. Apparently, before or after the end of the war a large number of Germans from the Africa Corps, for various reasons known only to themselves, had joined the French Foreign Legion. They must have had very good reason indeed to join a French unit, being aware of the great enmity that existed between the Germans and French. The fighting was between German and French, both wearing the same uniform. From what we saw before we left, I would assume that, it would be a long time before the place opened again for normal trading.

The next day the RAF flew us to Hong Kong. A few weeks later I bought a 27 ft yacht for six hundred pounds. Two friends and I spent some interesting times sailing around the Island. As a result three of us decided to sail back to England in the yacht. We started to plan for this and accrue the needed items for navigation etc. The Navy generously helped by supplying us with some of the equipment we needed. When the time for demobilisation neared the three of us approached the Air Commodore for release in Hong Kong. He was furious to know that we were willing to take such a risk. I thought back on my last 6 years with amusement. He immediately posted one of us to Japan, the other back to England and told me I would go back to England also but was given a week to sell the boat. My week was up. I had sold the boat and I was sent straight back to England where a few weeks later I was demobilised with the substantive rank of Flight Lieutenant.

You will recall that at about fifteen years of age my parents thought I needed glasses and took me to an optometrist. I was a shy introvert who spoke very little and never went to parties and had few friends. Yet in spite of my upbringing I had refused to wear the glasses. If I had worn them I would never have been accepted as a pilot in the Royal Air Force and I would not have undergone the experiences that have made me the confident and self-assured person that I am today. This story would never have existed and I would not have had the wonderful wife and family with which I have been blessed.

You Never Know

THE END
Philip Zeid. OBE FISP